I0415945

As It Happened

For 6 Gay Decades

by J.P. Johnson

Chapter 1 - The 1940's

There was a time when I thought that anyone over the age of 29 was an old person. Now that I am 62 years old, it is hard for me to think of myself as being old. When I reflect back on the things that I have done and the way my world has changed, it tends to suggest that I must be old. Over the many years, I have worked as an energetic youth in the farmers' fields of my home town and eventually found myself lecturing to a state wide meeting of superintendents of schools. Then I moved from the cold climate of the northeast and my dignified position in the administrative offices of the public schools to the tropical climate of the southeast and the somewhat controversial situation of owning a multimillion-dollar gay resort complex. The same personal characteristics which were once a source of embarrassment that I had to hide became my advertised claim to fame. Six decades provided enough time for me to have lived in at least three different worlds of places, people and social standards. Friends and associates from each of these periods have shared experiences with me that frequently resulted in a suggestion that I should write a book. Places and events from my past are stranger than science fiction to the people around me today, so I decided that it was time for me to write something down.

To start at the beginning, I have to go back to the year 1943. There are events from that time which still affect me more than what happens today, so I'll return to my memories and the things I was told about those years. It was a different world than the one we live in today. Cars were either black or gray and a photograph of them on the streets would clearly identify the time. Even the street lights, with their big reflector disk above an exposed light bulb, identified the 1940's.   Air-conditioning had been invented, but there were very few places where you could find it in use. The two-story homes with 10 foot ceilings and a third floor attic surrounded by shade trees were usually cool without air conditioning. A telephone call was a nickel and a loaf of bread was 15¢. No one was allergic to smoke and a pack of cigarettes was 17¢. If you made a 95¢ purchase, you could add a 5¢ pack of gum to make it an even dollar. There were no sales taxes to make it $1.06 with 94¢ in change.

A majority of the population lived in small towns and the people knew almost everyone in their town. Stores were operated by their owners and no one knew what it meant to ask for the manager. In fact, you were always talking directly to the owner on a first name basis. Credit cards had not been invented, but you could always put it on your bill and the amount would be added to your page in a notebook. The due date was when it had been a while since you last paid your bill. We refer to credit cards as plastic money and plastic was seldom used either. Things were made from real wood, glass, stone, metal, and ceramics.

A few homes had television sets and the owners had to be home on the nights that there was a broadcast which was either Milton Berle or wrestling.

Social life usually centered around a church or school. A sports enthusiast was someone who played baseball rather than someone who played the ESPN channel. Almost half of the population could play some type of musical instrument. Most gathering places had a piano and every group of people had someone who could play the piano. A group of kids would make a baseball diamond on any open field with four pieces of cardboard and play the game without a sponsor, youth director, physical exam, insurance policy or hold harmless document.

There was very little crime, but 90 percent of today's laws did not exist and were not needed in the absence of a dense population. It was a neighborly good deed to clear your property by burning leaves each fall. Your pets ran freely in the back woods rather than getting their exercise from short walks on a leash and there was no reason to invent the pooper-scooper. If everyone changed the oil in their own cars and dumped the old oil in back yard holes, it would still be less pollution than we get from what drips off of today's millions of cars. No household had two cars and many didn't have one. Women didn't drive and if a woman worked, it was an insult to her husband for not being able to support her.

Swimming pools were for the rich and famous, but people could swim in almost any pond, lake, river, or stream. There was very little pollution coming from the smaller population.

Trenton, the capitol of New Jersey, was in one of the most densely populated areas of the country and yet you could walk to the city limits and find yourself in farmlands and undeveloped countryside.

Nobody needed health insurance because lawyers had not made doctors and hospitals spend a fortune on malpractice insurance. People could afford to pay for an operation or any medical services that were needed. Lawyers seemed to know how to stay affluent without making 30% of a multi-million dollar malpractice claim.

It doesn't seem possible that things could have been so different a mere 60 years ago and I feel somewhat certain that I would not elect to trade the things that we lost from then, for the things that we gained in current times. I would still rather sit in a cool wooded area near a stream with a dozen friends drinking Iced Tea than to be in an air-conditioned, shopping center bar, drinking Budweisser from a frosted mug. Just as surely as I never thought Dick Tracy's wrist watch would ever be able to call his office, I never thought there would be a time when it would be necessary to pay a dollar for a bottle of clean drinking water. I am sure that I would trade my cellular phone for an opportunity to spend one day in the past, even if I was charged the taxes and license fees that would be required by today's world. It makes me wonder with trepidation about what the world will be like 60 years from now.

The war put a few hardships on people. Gasoline was rationed and it was difficult to get the ration stamps. There were things that you could not get because the labor force was serving in the military and many industrial plants were converted to the production of war supplies. Nobody minded hardships that had a good cause and it only lasted for a few years.

That was the world that I would be born into on October 24th, 1943. I have always felt that the person whom I would eventually become was seriously molded by the nature of those times and the events that took place then and in the few years preceding my birth. The truth about those years wasn't realized until I reached adulthood and assembled some facts into logical conclusions.

Chapter 2 - Family History

My mother had a brother who was a few years older and another brother who was many years younger. They were raised by my grandmother, a cleaning lady for a wealthy family in Princeton, New Jersey. My fine and upstanding, Christian family had a skeleton in their closet that remained hidden from me until I was 30 years old. After many years of seeing grandmom as a righteous and upstanding Christian person, I would eventually learn that my mother's youngest brother was actually only a half brother, fathered by a member of the household where my grandmother was employed. Grandmom was one of the few people in my entire life that showed me affection and love. I never held it against her for having a human flaw. It did teach me the possible errors in making assumptions about people, good or bad. I also thought that mom was just as righteous as grandmom and above doing anything indiscrete. If I come to what are reasonable conclusions, mom was just as human as her mother.

Mom was usually in the company of two very good girlfriends that were not exactly, conservative ladies from Hyannis Port. It was the beginning of World War II and the nearby army base of Fort Dix offered a ratio of men to women that had to be appealing to three not so conservative ladies. Mom frequently mentioned places that she had visited near the Fort Dix town of Wrightstown.

Dad was a New York boy stationed at Fort Dix. We see the New York City area as a major metropolitan site today, but dad's Long Island home of that time was surrounded by dairy farms and he was not really a city boy. His home was near a horse stable for polo ponies and that was his teenage hangout. Dad once told me that it was not good to be the middle brother because the oldest boy was the boss and the youngest boy was the baby and the middle boy had no advantages. The comment was a good description of his relationship to his brothers. He was much closer to his younger brother than the older brother.

This was the general information about what was to be the beginning of my family. There is a great deal of evidence that a few more details would make this a spicy story.

Mom was a few years older than dad and both of them seemed to avoid offering that information during my entire life. I was born in October of 1943, after dad had been shipped off to the war in Germany. My younger sister was born a year after he returned in 1945. He always treated her like his daughter, but he never made me feel like his son. She loved him and I feared him. I share too many of his characteristics not to be his son and have always looked for other reasons that we were so far apart. It might be that I should blame the war which kept him from seeing me until I was 2 years old. He did not know me as a baby and came home to a small boy at his house. Other times, I tried to associate some dates with a nine month period and determine if I was the cause of a shotgun wedding. Whatever the reason, my father and I avoided each other for 3 decades. It was worse than having been raised by a single parent because there was a combination of rejection and fear in my relationship to dad.

My father was the son of Swedish immigrants who came to this country through Ellis Island. Although they were both Swedish immigrants from the same area of Sweden, my grandmother and grandfather met and married in this country. Neither of them could speak a word of English and they had to survive using hand language until they taught themselves English. They came to this country at the wrong time because it is now necessary for me to learn Spanish to accommodate the current immigrants. Two-thirds of the employment ads in South Florida newspapers include the stipulation, must be bilingual. It is perfectly legal to discriminate against an English speaking American, if you do not mention their sex, color or religion. My current television service makes it possible for me to get Spanish subtitles on the English-speaking stations. There are so many Spanish speaking stations that I have noticed programs of interest on them, but there is no option to get English subtitles.

I am told that my grandfather was a big and easy going man that everybody loved. He was very skilled in carpentry and held a good job with the Steinway piano company. Mom always enjoyed telling people about the afternoon that grandpop took me down into their cellar and built a wooden wagon for me. It was all done with hand tools and even the round wheels were made of wood. I could be heard a block away when I was pulling the wooden-wheel wagon behind me. Life didn't treat him very well. They came to this country because of bad times in Sweden and they arrived here in time for the American depression. Shortly after the depression, all three of their sons served in the war. They raised my father and his two brothers in their home on Long Island and were grateful to this country for accepting them, even with the depression and war. They knew their obligations better than their rights.

I can hardly remember my grandfather and he probably could have been the one male influence in my life that would have changed the way I developed over the first 10 years. We went for walks together, every time my parents visited dad's old home in New York. I remember how impressed I was by a pedestrian bridge that crossed over a major highway to a cemetery. There was a candy store in the neighborhood that grandpop always chose as one destination for our walks. He enjoyed telling the shop owner that I was his grandson. My choice was always the bridge that let us look down on cars passing below. It wouldn't be long until grandpop would be making his last trip to that cemetery without me. He laid down on their living room couch, one afternoon, when I was about four years old. He told my grandmother that he didn't feel good and was going to the doctors the next day. My father said that if he was going to the doctors, he must be dying. A few weeks later, he died of cancer of the pancreas.

Dad frequently indicated that he was very close to his own father who idolized me as a grandson, but they didn't seem to share that opinion.

My mother's father was a tin smith. He worked in our town and I saw him all of my life, but never spoke to him. Mom never said much about him, but grandmom told us that he was a disgusting, dirty old man. My mother's oldest brother worked with him and they both seemed like good, hard working people. I stayed away from my grandfather because of my grandmother's comments, but when I learned about mom's younger brother, I wasn't sure that my grandfather was the bad half of that couple. We never spoke to mom's oldest brother who also lived in our town. Many years later, I found out that his wife made a drunken pass at my father during a New Years Eve party and our families stopped speaking.

Chapter 3 - The Building Blocks of my Character

My father's idea of constructive criticism was actually constant ridicule that was never interrupted by a complementary comment. Almost everything that he said to me was a warning to stop doing something or an instruction to do something better than the way I was doing it. This caused me to develop an inferiority complex by the time I reached elementary school. I avoided organized sports and most things competitive because I expected and feared failure. This developed into an admiration and consequently a desire for the men that I could not join as an equal and a friend. The public school system made it even worse by praising the same boys that I already admired and forcing me into the competitive situations where I would fail. I do recall having crushes on a few different girls during my youth and avoided pursuing the interests because of my inferiority complex. I feared inadequacy at performing my role in a heterosexual relationship.

So here I am, following the tradition of my mother's family and adding a skeleton to our closet. The psychologists and church leaders are constantly explaining the homosexual. Well, I've been there and done that and can lend them some information. No it is not a disease and they don't have to look for some bacteria that causes it. My medical records and physical examinations are very typical. There are no extra percentages of some hormone or missing chromosomes. Nobody else in my family was queer and I didn't inherit the trait. I sincerely think that it was learned and absolutely know that it can not be unlearned. You can raise a small tiger to become a friendly pet in the right atmosphere, but don't try to capture a mature tiger from the wild and teach it to be your next lap pet. I do honestly believe that I am gay because of my admiration for men which was created by my environment.

Among my gay friends, I saw a variety of influences that came to the same end result. Some of my extremely good looking gay friends were the product of escaping from women rather than admiring men. Extremely good looks can result in too many women making too many advances at too early of an age. It can create a gay boy who is looking to escape something that was forced upon him and find something that is desirably unavailable. Extremely domineering mothers will frequently create sons who never learn to make a decision on their own behalf and their subsequent lack of confidence in themselves is similar to my own inferiority complex. Regardless of what factors are present in developing the gay desires, my first hand experience and observations tell me that being gay is learned.

During my very young years, I did have an interest in girls and can recall having sexual fantasies about them. Those interests in girls were diminishing after I discovered an infatuation for a man named Earl, whom I saw at about age 10. He was a strikingly handsome, tall, blond, broad shouldered guy of about 25, who moved into a house a few blocks from my home. I imagined all sorts of reasons for him to be living alone in a three-bedroom house and realized that it made him extremely available for private encounters. It was exciting for me to just get a glimpse of him as he left his home or shopped in one of the local stores. In those days, it was assumed that 100 percent of the population was straight because anyone who was gay, had to stay in the closet. There was nothing that I could do about this infatuation for my tall blond man and desiring the unavailable made it even more enticing. I recall watching him get into his car and the memory brings back the same excitement that occurred nearly 50 years ago.

My father never invited me to do anything with him and he always wanted my sister to do everything with him. I can recall an occasion in my early years, when he took me to his place of work and left me in the car while he went to discuss something with his boss. The fact that he wanted me to stay in the car made me feel that he was embarrassed to show me as his son. The way that he treated me was probably the strongest influence over my becoming gay and ironically, being gay would be his idea of reason for embarrassment. I never let myself develop any feminine characteristics because I found them repulsive in men. Nobody could tell that I was a developing gay and I doubt if it had any affects on my father's original rejection of me.

Chapter 4 - The Homes of My Youth

Grandmom's employer was a very wealthy woman from Princeton, New Jersey. There may have been some obligation for her to assist my grandmother because of my mother's younger half brother. She paid mom's tuition to become a beautician. When I was born, mom was renting a large and beautiful home in the best part of town. She had a beauty shop in this house that she was sharing with my grandmother and uncle, who was only a few years older than me.

I cannot recall living in my first home, but I do

vividly recall our next home, even though I was less than five years old. I can only assume that mom moved from the nice house that she shared with grandmom into a small apartment with a store in front because dad returned from the war when I was 2 years old. The apartment was on a main street in the center of town and the store front made an excellent beauty shop. Surprisingly, I can remember some things that were very enjoyable about that location. Gustav Schmitz's bakery sold the best bread that I have ever eaten in a small store across the street. There were no preservatives in his baked goods and they would turn stale within a day, but the bread was so good that you could eat an entire loaf without even using butter. There was a grocery store next to the bakery. Mom could run across the street from her business to get boiled ham and bread for our lunches. There was a soda fountain two doors from the beauty shop that had a display case of penny candy. The owners of the soda fountain were a middle-aged couple that never had children of their own. They loved kids and never minded standing behind the glass candy case while we selected pieces of candy from the display dishes. It wasn't very profitable for them to spend 15 minutes for a 5¢ sale of candy, but they were financially secure and didn't need to make a profit. Our family sat on the front steps of the beauty shop during the early evening hours in the summertime. Friends and neighbors walked by and always spent a few minutes to talk about something. It was a very friendly and convenient place to live. My sister was just a baby and mom could take care of us while she was working because of the beauty shop and attached apartment. Every other aspect of the move was a significant step backward.

Strangely enough, I can remember almost every detail of that apartment even though I was less than five years old and we only lived there for a few years. There was indoor plumbing for a kitchen sink in the apartment and another sink in the beauty shop, but no bathroom. The beauty shop had a gas fired hot water heater and a kerosene stove for heat. The apartment had a coal stove in the living room that heated the small living room, kitchen, and two upstairs bedrooms. Dad partitioned off a small section of one bedroom and bought a chemical toilet to avoid continued use of the out house. He ran a hose from the beauty shop sink that had the only hot water to the cellar. They took a shower by turning on the beauty shop water and returning through the apartment to the cellar, where there was a wooden rack covering the dirt floor under the water from the beauty shop hose. The apartment even gave me the experience of knowing how an ice box works because we didn't have a refrigerator. That explains why I said everything else was a step backward. Dad came from a normal home in Long Island and mom had been living in a beautiful home in our town until this move.

The amazing part for me is the fact that I can even remember the furniture in that apartment. There are things of importance that I have completely forgotten and yet other insignificant events are as vivid as if they had happened this morning. We were coming down the stairway one morning with mom following me. She tripped at about five steps from the bottom and we both went forward into a table at the bottom of the stairs. We were lying on the floor with a broken leg from the table and I clearly recall asking my mother why she did that. She obviously did not intend to do it and started laughing at my question. What made me remember that silly event from the age of three?

Because it was a business, we had one of the first air conditioners in the beauty shop. Dad always accused me of liking to push buttons and I guess that is true because I can remember the controls on the air conditioner, the knob and the settings on the kerosene heater and the old black telephone that was connected to a large steel box on the wall.

One Christmas, dad had assembled a small train set in the beauty parlor as my present. He and my uncle played with it as much as I did and it grew each year with more trains as Christmas presents until it was an impressive set during my teenage years. My generous mother gave it to one of her customers who had a son when I was in college and that really upset me. It would be worth a considerable amount of money today and I would keep it for memory sake because it was something that gave me pleasurable time.

Kids must have been much more intelligent in

those days because we were allowed to walk around the city streets and play without supervision at a preschool age. I must admit that it was somewhat like having hundreds of babysitters because you were constantly in the presence of people who knew you and your parents. There were main streets right next to the sidewalks where we played. There was a bridge over a large lake that was a major attraction and nobody drowned. Dad always kept a gun in his bedroom and we knew that it was too dangerous to touch. The rules were simply to be home for meals and when it got dark. Although many people would argue the idea, there was a big difference in the kids of that time. Our elders were always addressed as Mr. or Mrs. Even the very private conversations would seldom include a swearword. If we were punished for breaking a rule at school, we would never mention it at home because there would be a follow-up punishment rather than the more modern trend of suing the school. Kids generally did what was right because it was right and not necessarily because they were being supervised.

The city was completely surrounded by farms. Farms had open fields for planting which were bordered by wooded areas and the lake. Five local businessmen formed a company and purchased one of the farm plots adjacent to the city limits for the development of a housing complex. They laid a perimeter road and a few streets through the complex. Another local contractor purchased two lots from them and built two speculation homes on the outer edge of the complex. Dad purchased one of those homes during our third year in the apartment. They continued to rent the storefront for a few more years and eventually moved the beauty parlor to the cellar of their new house.

It was shortly after grandpop died and dad's mother was living with us in the new house. She contributed construction money for the completion of a second floor bedroom. The old theory that two women cannot live under the same roof was accurate and she was only with us for a short time before returning to a New York City apartment. In fairness to my parents, it was grandmon that created problems and her construction money was returned to her before the mutually approved plan sent her back to New York.

The house was a small Cape Cod house with a single car garage that would probably be considered low middle income. None of the development houses were built yet and dad's house was across an open field from town, adjacent to a wooded area. Even though it was only a few blocks from center city, all of our friends referred to us as having moved out in the sticks. Our lot was gigantic by today's standards and we had miles of wooded area to explore as kids. It was fun to make trails through the woods and bridges over the streams.

The local lake would freeze approximately three times a year and the whole community would be together ice skating. The city provided lighting on the lake at the end near town and the skating parties continued until midnight. You could skate away from town and past our development on to streams that continued for miles into the woods. There was seldom a person that you didn't know even when there were more than 200 people on the lake. Ice skating was something that I did much better than the boys who were our star athletes at school. Their parents taught them to play the popular ball games, but they didn't have the same advantage in ice skating. We had a popular game that was played regularly and this was one place that I always joined in. Everyone would stand behind a line on one side of the lake except one person. The remaining person would stand in the center of the lake and shout "goosey" to make everyone cross to a safety line on the opposite side of the lake. Dad always laughed at our New Jersey game and asked my mother why we used the word "Goosey". It was a good question and we did not have a good answer. Anyone touched by the person standing in the center had to join the center group. Eventually, there would only be one person left to cross the lake and that was the winner. It frequently got rougher than football, but our winter clothes seemed to protect us better than a football uniform. Girls and guys of all ages played. We were just a little more careful when we tagged a girl or someone small and they were usually out of the game before it got rough. The older I got, the more I enjoyed the game because I was starting to enjoy being attacked by some of the guys. The Methodist minister's son was an extremely good-looking guy who was a few years younger than me. It was the time when people were streaking and he streaked his high-school graduation. I hated going to my own graduation, but I'm sorry I missed his. He was playing the game on the lake one afternoon and I was in the center. There was no way that he was going to get across the lake because I was going to dive at him for one reason or another. He was skating hard to get away from me and I kept going faster until I hit him in the side and landed on top of him. We were both going so fast that he broke the blade off of his ice skate. We laid on the ice laughing at his funny looking ice skate and I was right where I wanted to be. His graduation streaking incident had repercussions that affected his ability to enter college and may have been instrumental in his father's transfer to another city. It was one of those situations when you wished you could do something about it because he was really a nice kid in addition to his good looks. Gay people were obviously not the only ones that were victims of the times, because the Greek and Roman cultures would have made nude statues of that great body and placed them in the most conspicuous locations.

There was an old mill on the Lake that actually functioned by a water wheel until I was about 10 years old. It was an amazing thing to have seen it work with all of the wooden drive shafts, wooden gear wheels, and gigantic drive belts. It was eventually electrified and is currently converted to stores. The lake seldom froze very hard over the area of where a concentrated flow

21

of water went into the mill rush. One afternoon, a young woman was putting her ice skates on and her five year old son walked out over the mill rush. I saw where he was going from the bridge and ran down to stop him. The ice broke and I got there just in time to grab his hand as he was going under the water. I wasn't even 10 years old myself and I had saved somebody's life, but in all of the subsequent confusion and concern about the boy, there was no acknowledgement for my good deed. It didn't really bother me because I had a feeling of satisfaction that couldn't be enhanced by anyone's complementary words.

Most of the boys in town were in the Boy Scouts and I joined too. Their meeting place was in a barn on the same property that my mother rented when I was born. One of the wealthiest families in town had purchased the house and offered use of the barn to the Boy Scouts. Walking through the property always made me wonder how my mother could have afforded to live in a home which was now occupied by millionaires.

It is hard for me to figure out who actually was in charge of our family during those school years in the development house. At the time, it seemed obvious that dad was the controlling person. He was the voice of authority, but I later realized that he only exercised authority to enforce principles that were really my mother's ideals.

Our family was typical in some regards and very

atypical in others. Mom worked in her beauty shop at a time when most women did not work and that never bothered my father. My parents met their obligations to raise their children and live according to the acceptable social standards of the time. We always had adequate shelter, healthy food, presentable clothing and a Christian education. We never had the slightest display of affection. I never saw my father kiss my mother or heard him say anything that was of an affectionate nature, even at the party of their 25th wedding anniversary. I wouldn't dare say anything bad about her in his presence, but there was a total lack of any emotion in our family. Many years later, I went home with a very good friend of mine and his children ran to the door to meet him. He picked each of them up and hugged and kissed them. At first I thought that he was very unusual in that display of affection, but I came to realize that I was the one who was very unusual in not recognizing that as a common greeting. It certainly wasn't common in my background.

Mom never fought with Dad and seldom disagreed with him. She would just agree with what ever he said and totally ignore it anyway. She helped with local church dinners and if they ran out of any thing, they always sent my mother to the store because they knew she would donate whatever she bought. Dad told her that they were using her and if she was going to continue doing it, at least get a receipt so they could take it off their income tax. She agreed, continued shopping for them, and never got a receipt. He would eventually give up because she would never argue the issue and never change. Everything that they did was by mutual agreement. Dad asked mom to go car shopping with him and she didn't want to go because she knew nothing about cars. She had to go because he would not buy a car without mom's approval.

Chapter 5 - School Days,

School buses were provided to homes that were more than 2 miles from the school and we were 1.9 miles from school. Mom always drove my sister and I plus a few neighbors to school in the morning, but we walked home unless the weather was extremely bad.

I should have started elementary school at the age of 5. Mom pushed to get me into school at age 4 because my birthday would be two months after the beginning of the school year. It was not a good decision for me because it meant that I would be almost a year younger than my classmates throughout school. My psychological feeling of inferiority was going to be a physical reality because I would always be approximately a year less mature than my classmates. That was definitely detrimental to me.

The contractors finished the development houses within a year or two and I had many classmates in my neighborhood. They were all a low middle income type of housing and we were stereotyped with the distinguishing characteristic of the development kids. The doctors, lawyers, undertaker and successful business people all lived in large homes on the north end of the main street in town. The kids from that area were usually the class presidents and honor students. We supplied the ball teams and were the dumb jocks. I was on the wrong end of town, but I wasn't alone and we all survived our place in the population.

My uncle, grand mom's illegitimate son, was a senior in the high-school when I was in the eighth grade. He won a new car on the Jersey shore boardwalk and he drove to school from the house that grand mom had rented for them after dad came home and they left the house shared with mom. I thought that we were going to have a year of free rides home with Uncle Tom, but it never seemed to happen. Although we became very friendly in future years, his attitude was typical of a senior dealing with an eighth grader at that time. One of the girls in my class was several years older than me because she had been kept back a few times. She thought that my Uncle Tom was extremely handsome and I told him about her. They started dating and eventually were married. My Aunt Bertha was also my classmate. He joined the Navy after graduating from high school and was away for 20 years. Then he returned with a Navy pension and we became very friendly. Much to my surprise, he had known for years that he was an illegitimate child. My mother told me when I was an adult and I realized that I should have known too. It was just that I never thought my grandmother could do such a thing and never really questioned the fact that my uncle's first and middle names were the full name of grandmon's, employer's brother. It might have been a situation of rape and my faith in grandmon could have been justified, but that will never be known.

After becoming a teenager and entering high school in the late 1950's, I encountered a few effeminate boys whom everybody assumed were gay. Although it was my first opportunity to share my own experience, the fact that they were feminine was a turn off to me. I liked men and they acted like women, so they could not satisfy my desire. Our learned colleagues, who have analyzed the gay population, have concluded that homophobes are frequently closet case homosexuals who are denying their own identity. This is one conclusion that I can agree with because I conspicuously rejected the obviously feminine boys more aggressively then the rejections made by straight guys. Not unlike the described homophobes, I felt all of the attractions that should identify me as gay, but I had not told myself the simple statement, "I am gay ". I wasn't really sure that I was gay because I was infatuated with a girl that lived a few blocks from my home and very jealous when she showed an interest in other guys. We were playing in the hay loft of a local dairy farm and stacked the bales of straw to create a little house. The privacy of the situation offered an opportunity and created an irresistible desire for some type of heterosexual sex. Although nothing physical happened, I do remember the excitement of the moment with an awareness that I had an interest in a girl at about age 13.

The society of the times made it clear that gay was inferior and a gay person was forced to renounce it or evade the question. It was all actually part of the developing gay person. First, we renounced it to ourselves and when that was no longer possible, we only renounced it to others. Eventually, we could not build a case for denial and moved on to evading questions by changing the subject or attacking the interrogator with answers such as "why are you interested" or "Is that what you need".

I never did get to meet my tall handsome blond. He married a girl from the neighborhood and moved to a neighboring city. They say that sex isn't everything and for a gay person living in the 1950's, that was an understatement. Sex wasn't possible. The good thing about Earl moving away is that I never saw him get old. He will always be a great looking guy to me.

There was one occasion when I was nearly raped by two guys. One of them was nice looking and the other was at least average. Although it was frightening at the time, I have always been sorry that they did not finish their attempt and I frequently fantasized about what it would have been like to have had sex with them. They were seniors in high school and I was in the seventh grade. One of them had a pregnant girlfriend and was obviously, sexually experienced. We were all attending a Thanksgiving dinner on the first floor of our local Grange Hall. The building had a second floor auditorium that was not in use. Curious to see the auditorium, I went up into the dark second-floor. The two high-school seniors were already upstairs. They told me to take my clothes off and my reaction was fear because I was out numbered, out sized, and sexually unaware of what might happen. Little did they know, that either one of them could have talked me into what they wanted, in a friendly conversation. I threatened to shout to the room full of people downstairs and they walked away. Now, I regret that it turned out that way. It might have been one of the best days of my life. I wasn't Catholic and didn't have a priest, so I needed them. Society doesn't think kids should have sex, but I think that is cruel and a waste. Let's face it, sex starts going down hill after 25 and if you wait until you're 21, you only get 4 good years. There was a time when people only lived to 40 and girls were expected to be married at 15. Did we have to go from one extreme to the other?

My best two friends in high school were straight and masculine. One of them was having sex with a girl that lived near me and everyone knew about it. Her yearbook comment said that she was "most likely to put out" and I was never sure how that slipped through. Could her parents and the school advisors interpret that to mean anything other than the insult that I saw? My two friends were nice looking and I would have enjoyed more than the platonic relationship that we had. They were average students and not members of the sports stars, but they did make it easy for me to stay in the closet during my high-school years. We were friendly enough for them to accept the fact that I was gay, but the attitude of the times made it too risky to chance exposure.

My parents made the same mistake that most middle-class parents make. They demanded good high-school grades and insisted on my devoting time to home work. That made school work seem like punishment or the enemy of my potentially pleasurable existence. This error is still practiced by middle-class families and somebody should educate the parents. Students who enjoyed studying had parents who would ask what today's homework assignment was and continue with enthusiastic remarks such as, " I remember that, let me see if I can still do it ". Parents need to make school work seem better than going to the movies rather than worse than two years at Alcatraz. Consequently, I devoted very little time to studying and maintained an average grade. I must have been above average intelligence to pass my courses without studying and it would have lessened my rejected son, inferiority complex to have been an honor student.

Chapter 6 - The Jersey Shore

Fortunately for us, Dad was raised near the shore on Long Island and he enjoyed swimming in the ocean. My entire family enjoyed the Jersey shore and access to that recreation was one of the few things that I had over my friends. It started as day trips to the beach on weekends and eventually resulted in our owning a beach house. Ocean swimming was a recreation that I truly enjoyed and the fact that beaches are full of men in bathing suits was completely ignored until after I graduated from high school.

There were a few years when we rented apartments for a week of beach vacation at the end of August. The water never got above 70 degrees and August was the best month for swimming. Sand on the New Jersey beaches is soft and white as bleached sugar. The waves rise high and are great for surfing. The undertow was strong, but it never bothered me because I realized that it would only pull you to the beginning of deep water and then you could easily get free. People that fought the undertow were the ones that would drown because you can't swim against it.

In the mid-1950s, a family in our home town was selling a beach house that they had built. My father saw it as a good investment opportunity and negotiated a purchase. I thought that it was the greatest thing that ever happened to us, but would soon learn how dad could screw that up. Every time we went to the beach house, dad had a new project for me to work on. We changed the door sills, tiled the kitchen and bathroom floors, changed all of the plumbing so that the water drained toward the rear of the house, sealed the roof tiles, painted the exterior, replaced screens on the side porch and so on. I was better off during the days of our weekend trips to the beach because I was swimming then and the new situation put me right next to the water with tasks that kept me from swimming. The beach house was rented during the summer with receipts that paid the mortgage. Guests arrived each Saturday and we went to the Jersey shore on Saturdays to clean the house for our next tenants. The trip home usually included a stop at some roadside hot dog stand. One of the little roadside refreshment stand businesses, very near our home, was constructing a swimming pool. The owners became familiar with us as regular customers and when the pool was finished, they stopped at our house on their way to the park and picked us up for a day in the pool. Many of our friends from town would be there every day and it became our summer home from the age of seven until it closed when we were adults.

Chapter 7 - The Picnic Park Swim Club

The owners of the park were twin brothers that ran it with their families. I became almost as much a member of their families as my own. I started working for them when I was old enough to get working papers. They made me take the Red Cross life-saving course so that I could be their lifeguard, but I did everything including cutting lawns, working in the refreshment stand, and even babysitting their children. When I was old enough to start driving a car, I visited them at their homes and still remain friendly with them after all these many years.

It was a place where I met several other people who also became very good friends. A friend of theirs named Bud was a race horse driver that lived near me. I became friendly with him and his family through our meetings at the park. Bud raced horses at tracks that were hundreds of miles apart and he was constantly on the road. When I became old enough to drive, I started going to the track with him because he wanted someone to do the driving and I enjoyed the special privileges that he could get for me. It was a great experience to enter the race track through the owner's gate and go over to the stadium with a clubhouse pass. I became friendly with many famous people and really enjoyed the experience. Bud topped off the evenings by always wanting to stop at some club. He knew where they had great entertainers in every city where he raced. It was really special when we went to a place that had lines of people waiting to get in and we would be called to the front because somebody recognized him as a celebrity. He knew the twins from the park because they all went to high school together.

There was a horse farm a few miles down the road from the park and the people from the farm were also part of our picnic park friends. We sometimes borrowed equipment from them if we needed a tractor or other farm tool. During my college years, they hired a farm manager from Texas named Will. At this point in my life, I was very much aware of the fact that men interested me more than women and he sure was a man.

I'm not sure if men do something for jeans or jeans do something for men, but I am sure that the combination is very appealing to me and he always wore tight jeans. We became very good friends in a non sexual way, but I sure wouldn't have minded adding sex to our relationship.

It was a breeding farm for standard bred race horses and I took advantage of several opportunities to watch the breeding. They had a special barn just for breeding that included a laboratory with medical supplies and sterilization equipment. It was somewhat dangerous because the large animals were very difficult to control during their sexual excitement. A strap similar to a dog collar with an attached rope was placed on a front foot of the mare. The rope would be pulled over her back to lift one of her feet off the floor. Standing on 3 feet made it impossible for her to kick. Then her tail would be wrapped with gauze and the genitals of both horses were washed with sterilizing soap. With all things prepared, the stud would be led over to the mare and the next few minutes were very dangerous. His front legs would be flying high and wide while Will was right there holding the mare's foot off of the floor. Will usually had to reach in and help in the aiming process. The stud was finished in less than a minute. Modern farms use artificial insemination because it is much safer for the valuable mares.

Trotter race tracks did not use a horse's month of birth in determining age. All of the breeding

33

was done in the first part of the year because foals were born at 12 months and a horse born in December would be considered one year old a month later. Breeding continued until the veterinarian found a fodical on the ovaries of the mare. Perrine, the veterinarian, was at the farm at least once a week to check the mares. He stacked two bales of straw behind her to protect himself from being kicked. Wearing a long plastic glove that went up to his shoulder, he would reach shoulder deep into the mare's anus and feel for a fodical on her ovaries. It didn't seem to hurt them and nothing seemed to bother Perrine. He was operating on a horse that had a hernia and ashes from his cigar fell into the incision. I was upset over ashes in the cut and he told me to stop worrying because those ashes were sterilized at 1000 degrees. I always remember his remark when somebody says that an ashtray is dirty. It is actually very sterile. The horse never got an infection and I had to assume that he was correct.

Perrine gave the horses worm medication and the straw from the stables was filled with worms. A Pennsylvania mushroom farm made regular trips to the horse farm for the dirty straw from the stables. It would be spread over the mushrooms as fertilizer. When they wanted the straw that was filled with worms, my ability to eat mushrooms had ended.

Will's wife was from a prominent New York family and they were extreme opposites. They met while she was working for an Air lines in

Texas and it had to have been a purely physical attraction. She wanted to go to art shows and museums while he wanted to sit on the back porch and drink Hamms beer. We all went to the world's fair in New York and had to go through the cultural exhibits for Will's wife before we could see things that interested Will and me. She took a job that caused her to do some occasional work in a neighboring city. It was only an hour's drive, but she sometimes spent the night because she had a boyfriend there. She would tell Will that a belt broke on the car, but he checked the car and didn't see any changed belts. Will, gave me one of her night gowns that had a stain on it and asked me to take the nightgown to college and find out what was in the stain. I laughed and said that I couldn't take a nightgown into college and do that, so he cut a big circle out of the nightgown and had a circle of stained cloth. I still wouldn't take it to the college. A few days later, we were all sitting in the kitchen and she was removing laundry from the clothes dryer. She held up the nightgown and said, what the hell happened to this? I had to leave the room because I could not keep myself from laughing. She followed me and said that I knew something because I was laughing. I said that if I was going to wear a nightgown, it would be helpful to have a pee hole like that and I wish I needed one that big. She accepted that as my reason for laughing and I got away with it.

One summer, Will's nephew visited for two months. Johnny, the nephew, was like an early birthday present for me. He wasn't what I would consider exceptionally handsome and he wasn't unattractive either. His appeal came from his very masculine nature even though he didn't look like a body builder. The only thing that he missed while visiting New Jersey, was participating in the summer rodeos in Texas and he looked like the guys you see in rodeos. We spent most of the summer together and had a great time. The swim club was our daily routine unless I took him to the Jersey shore. He wrestled with me in the water and I was elated to have a young Texan stud climbing all over me. I'll never forget the night that we went to a drive in movie and saw "Mad Mad Mad World". The movie had some funny parts, but Johnny found everything funny and talked about that movie for the rest of the summer. I think that I laughed at John more than the movie and I am sure that I enjoyed John more than the movie.

I graduated from college the following year and immediately got into a car and drove all the way to Texas. John's small remote town was accessed by driving through a creek bed and you couldn't go there if it was raining. Everything from banks to beer was named Lone Star. Lone Star beer was treated more like food than alcohol and could be purchased by almost anyone from every store that sold food or convenience goods. Pickup trucks had shotguns hanging in the window behind the driver. Johnny explained that you needed the shotguns because there were rattlesnakes in the fields. We went into a field to look at his horse and I never took my eyes off of the ground. He took me to a dude ranch to see a staged gunfight that they performed for tourists. Then we took a ride down into Mexico to see a border town. He and his grandmother, Will's mother, lived together in a nice ranch house. John and I shared the fact that our fathers showed no interest in us and that might have added to my feeling of attachment to John. His grandmother was a very funny and friendly lady. They seemed to get along with each other better than most families. I was glad to see that he had someone who cared about him and it did not surprise me to discover that it would be a grandmother. She told me that she had been sick for three days because there was a scorpion in her shoe that stung her when she put it on.

I was surprised to see how different things were in another area of my own country. Not only the rattlesnakes and scorpions, but even the language was different. What we would call a paper bag was a sack to them. A New Jersey 50 pound sack of potatoes was a bag of potatoes in Texas. If you asked for a soda, they would ask you what kind of ice cream because what we would call soda was pop in Texas. The best part was sleeping in the same bed with John. Nothing happened, but this was the closest I ever came to something happening. On second thought, I can't say that nothing happened because it was a special excitement to know that he was a few inches from me in bed.

It was really disturbing when I saw John leave the farm on the year before my trip to Texas because I assumed that I would never see him again. Having seen him helped me to get over that feeling of permanent loss and it was a worthwhile trip. I never saw John again, but knowing that I could was enough to end my need to visit again.

Will eventually asked me to take a ride with him and show him the city where his wife was working. I really did not want to get involved, but he made it obvious that I was not going to evade his request. We found his car parked outside of a bar in the neighboring city. He went in and found his wife sitting on a man's lap at the bar. The only thing that he did was to let her know that she had been caught. We went back out to the car and returned to the farm where he packed his clothes and left for Texas. I never saw him again.

If I am talking about picnic park friends, I must include Robert. He was a young fellow that was just starting to work in his father's undertaker business. The father had a very typical undertaker's personality, but the son Robert, was much worldlier. I received a telephone call from him at about 7:00 p.m. and he asked what I was wearing. A gay man might be interested in what another man was wearing, but he had no idea that I was gay and I knew that he was not, so this was a very strange question. I assumed that he was up to something and decided to answer his strange question with an even stranger answer. I was standing at the phone in my underwear and told him that I was wearing a suit and tie. I was never so happy to have told a lie because he was inviting me to a "come as you are" party. My answer was so perfect for the unexpected question that I had to put on a suit and tie and go to the party. I went down the dark hallway from the funeral parlor to his apartment and found several friends already in the living room. One of the woman owners of the park asked me if I saw the woman in the hallway. She said that she would not have come if it had been her because the poor woman was totally naked. After the party got going, we pulled Robert to the side and ask him who the woman was that showed up naked. He went out into the hallway and came back laughing with a mannequin under his arm. It was a store mannequin with a Brillo pad in the crotch. Awhile later, someone remarked that Bud and his wife did not show up for the party. We were not going to let him get away with it. We put the mannequin in the trunk of a car and drove three cars of people to Bud's House. He lived just outside of town, over the crest of a hill and across the street from a cornfield. We parked our cars on the opposite side of the hill and in front of his neighbor's so that he would not see them. Most of us went into the corn field to hide while Robert took the mannequin from his trunk and put it on Bud's front porch. He rang the doorbell and then hid. Bud's wife answered the door and started screaming to Bud that there was a naked woman on the porch. Bud came to the front door at about the same time as the police arrived. The stunt was meant for Bud, but his poor neighbor saw us and called the police because somebody was taking a body out of a trunk in front of her house. Thank God for small towns where the chief of police knew all of us and was probably one of the people who did not show up for the party. Robert was a character, but he was a nice guy and made a very sincere apology to the neighbor that we scared.

Chapter 8 - Rider College

Rider College, now Rider University, was a prestigious, private college in the North Jersey area of Princeton University and Rutgers University. In 1961, the year that I graduated from high school, Rider College opened an expansive new campus that housed four times its previous student body. Professors criticized the college for lowering their entrance requirements to fill the new campus. The professors did not lower their course standards and the result was an extraordinary percentage of failures. It worked to my advantage because my high-school grades were not indicative of my potential and this made it possible for me to enter an exclusive college with my grades.

Nobody from my family had ever graduated from college and a very small percentage of the society went to college in those days. For the first time in my life, I had a feeling of superiority that gave me the impetus to study and to become an honor student. The experience was building my self confidence that had been stripped away by my father's attitude toward me. I was very popular and had a number of extremely good-looking college hunks as friends, but maintained my gay secret. It was very difficult on an occasion in our junior year in college. I invited a large group to join me at my parent's beach house that spring. There was only one small bathroom, so the women used one-bedroom and the men used another bedroom to change into bathing suits. If it wasn't hard enough to endure being in a room full of naked college hunks, the best looking one made it even worse by saying that he did not have a bathing suit and wanted me to cut the legs off his pants. He stuck a leg up for me to cut them while he was wearing them and I sure did accommodate his request. As I cut to the middle of the front of his jeans, he told me to be careful not to cut anything but the jeans, so I grabbed his manhood and lifted it out of the way. He thought it was funny and I thought it was fantastic. If anyone had grabbed me in that location, my excitement would have shown. He was the one being grabbed and I was the one getting excited. The reason that he didn't have a bathing suit was that he still had one more examination to take and planned on studying at the beach. His dorm room was cleaned out and he was wearing his only available clothes. The college did not permit shorts and he had to take an exam the next day, so we put the legs back on his jeans with safety pins. It sure did look funny, but satisfied the rules of the college.

Mom went to high school with the daughter of our local Cadillac dealer. Jean taught music in our school system and gave me piano lessons until she married the girl's physical education teacher. They moved into a house near my college and found new teaching jobs in an area where they were not known as lesbians. I visited them a few times because they were near the college and always welcomed company. I have always believed that your immune system provides the best cure for diseases and you can psychologically control its ability to work. Jean was an excellent example of proof. She was always afraid of cancer and had the routine pap smears and chest exams. She died of cancer at age 40. She convinced herself that she would get cancer and did.

My college graduation ceremony was the first occasion that my father ever showed a degree of satisfaction in me. His brothers were at the service and none of them had graduated from college.

Our entire college group graduated and we lost contact except for articles that we read about each other in the Rider University annual publication. I left Rider College with a feeling of superiority that was about to grow as I became president of a church board during the construction of an entirely new church, was elected to president of a teachers' association where I worked, and traveled in the company of some very prominent people in the race horse industry.

There were a few years in the early 1960's, when

dad stopped renting the house and we started to use it for more than the one week previously reserved each season. The summer of 1965, I had graduated from college and the beach house was empty all summer. We had always used the public beach, but there was a club with a private beach adjacent to ours and I thought it would be special to be a member. It was a place where I saw people having fun for many years and I could never get in. I joined the club with beach, bar, and locker room privileges. I had also turned 21 and could join the party at the bar. I was so interested in being an accepted member of the crowd, that I continued to overlook the fact that there were many, good looking and scantily clothed men. Drinking became the new focus and led to playing volleyball with friends and employees at the bar. Everyone eventually knew me on a first name basis and I felt like an accepted member of the crowd. They finally awakened my gay awareness on an afternoon when the ocean was too cold for swimming. It was the normal practice to cool off by jumping into the ocean after playing volleyball, but the cold ocean caused all of us to go into the locker room and shower. The room full of naked, young men made me want to stare in directions that I should not be looking and I had an entirely new attitude toward these guys that were my friends. I had seen men in bathing suits on the beach since I was five years old and was conditioned to think nothing of it, but that was all about to change.

Chapter 9 - My First Job

The decision to become a teacher was one of the wrong choices that I made during my lifetime. I never enjoyed standing in front of a group and speaking. It was always a pleasure for me to do things that produced some end result which was tangible evidence of having accomplished something. The successes of a teacher would be found in the subsequent successes of his or her students many years after they leave the class and frequently, never to be known by the teacher. It was a double edged sword. I really didn't want teaching and teaching didn't need me. There was a shortage of teachers at the time that I decided to become one, but too many people decided to fill that shortage and the situation reversed by the time that I graduated from college.

The college placement office could not find a position for me in the area of my home. This was a blessing in disguise because it caused me to move into our beach house and take a position at the Jersey shore. Total independence made it one of the best years of my life. It is hard for me to believe that the annual salary was $5,400 and I lived rather well on that amount.

My father picked two cars that I used in my 4 year commute to Rider College. The first was a four-cylinder English Vaux Hall and the second was a six-cylinder Chevrolet with power glide. They were both gutless wonders of the cheapest makes available in the 1960's. My closest friend at college had a new Pontiac Grand Prix. It was

one of the first sports models that had bucket
seats, shift on the console, and a big eight
cylinder engine. One of the girls in my home
town was also going to Rider College and we car
pooled. She had a new eight cylinder Buick.
Another college friend had a red, Ford
convertible with an eight cylinder engine. To a
bunch of college kids, the eight cylinders was a
big thing. I surely wasn't one who needed one
more thing to support my inferiority complex,
but true to form, my father came through with
his six-cylinder cars that kept me one step down
the ladder from my friends. So, the first thing
that I did after getting a job was to buy an eight
cylinder Buick convertible. The experience had
a lasting effect on me because I spent the next 30
years buying the most expensive model, high
powered cars that I could possibly finance. Two
more cylinders on my college Chevy would
probably have made me a normal car buyer.
The ironic thing was that my six cylinder Chevy
got terrible gas mileage because of the loose
transmission.

The freedom of living alone at the beach house
was unbelievable. I had lived my entire life in a
small town where my mother owned the beauty
shop and my father worked for the city.
Everyone knew everything and everybody. I can
remember having purchased a pack of cigarettes
for a friend of mine at about age 15. We were on
the opposite side of town, but word got back to
my mother and the stern greeting that I got upon
arriving home was, "I want to talk to you ". I
couldn't even be known by my own name until

another generation had passed and my mother's friends would no longer be the school teachers and business owners. Until then, I would continue to be Loretta's son. Now, I was in an entirely new world. Everything was going to be an exciting discovery. When I walked through the front doors of a business, I had no idea of what to expect on the inside. I could go into a bar, which would have been a family taboo, and have no concern over who saw me going in. There was the possibility of meeting sexy people, nice people, fun people, as well as the usual run of dull people and nasty people to avoid. The new experiences were so much fun that I even told a gang of people that my name was Robert so that I could be totally rid of my past and begin a whole new experience. It was the ultimate freedom to be able to pick your own name at age 22.

I knew that the first day of teaching was going to be a traumatic experience of stage fright. Although I wasn't too comfortable about public speaking, I was smart enough to figure out a way to get through it. I just passed the buck by making everyone stand up and introduce themselves. Once everyone else had spoken, it was easy to finish up the remaining minutes. Any time that I wanted to get off the stage, I would come up with a question and put someone else on stage. After a while, I didn't need to use my little trick. In fact, I became president of the teachers' association and was quite relaxed in addressing 100 professional teachers at the association meetings.

It was the '60s and I had to remain very professional and in the closet, but I have to admit that I did enjoy some of the male students at the high-school. I had to be very careful not to treat them differently or even glance at them for a second longer than required in my duties as a teacher. The same thing was true about fellow staff members. I'll never forget the math teacher who lived in an apartment at the end of my street. My studies at Rider College included a federal tax course and the math teacher needed help with his income tax preparation. By appointment, I went to his apartment and found him dressed in a pair of jockey shorts. His taxes were simple because all of his income was on W-2 forms and I could save him some money because multiple employers had resulted in an overpayment of Social Security taxes. After we finished the tax forms, he asked me if I wanted to play cards. I laughed and said that we couldn't play strip poker because he wasn't dressed for staying in the game very long. Actually, I would have let him win at strip poker because I was enjoying the jockey shorts and wouldn't want the game to end too quickly. As usual, nothing happened, but that was the extent of gay sex in those days.

Jack B., the president of the board of education was my former eighth grade school teacher. It was somewhat obvious that he was gay, but a fat, bald, not very handsome man. Jack would sometimes speak Latin and was proud of having studied to become a priest. He never told me why he became a school teacher instead of a priest, but he did tell me that his mother always tried to control his life and that was why he lived on the east coast while his mother was in California. The domineering mother was adequate explanation for Jack's gay characteristic. This was the first time that the '60s worked in my favor. He had to be very professional and in the closet. His wife and adopted teenage son were very friendly and a lot of fun. The circumstances made it safe for me to visit them and help out with his tax accounting business. The husband and wife relationship appeared to be one of the familiar arrangements for hiding in the gay closet. Their arguments were nasty, but sometimes funny. She once remarked that she was going to the beauty shop for an hour and he told her that she needed to stay all day. We were sitting at the kitchen table one Sunday morning and he asked her how much it would cost him to get rid of her for a week. She said $500. He took out his checkbook and wrote a check for $500. She took the check and left. Two nights later, she showed up at the house and he told her that he still had 5 more days left. She said that she ran out of money and the contract wasn't any good because it was done on a Sunday. He asked her how much more she needed, but she didn't leave this time.

Chris, the adopted son, was attractive and fairly mature at the time he was adopted. I always wondered if his stepfather was doing a good job of staying in the closet when it came to providing a home for an attractive male that was no baby.

His tax business appeared to be very successful because they had a beautiful home with his and hers Cadillacs in the garage. They ate most of their meals in fine restaurants and frequently took me with them. A few years after I left the area, he was arrested for selling drugs and I was never sure that the tax business was their real source of income when I was there. I tend to think that he used drug sales to stay in contact with guys rather than make money. Later rumors were that he had a heart attack and never went to court. Health problems kept him out of court until he died approximately a year later. I have always wanted to know where his wife and son went, but I never heard from them again.

Chapter 10 - Moving Back to Dad's House

The city was about to build a sewage plant two blocks from our beach house, so dad sold it and I had to move. There was no way for him to know that the sewer plant would come and property values would go up anyway. They pumped sewage from inland cities and sometimes opened the bypass valves because they couldn't handle the volume. Raw sewage went directly into the ocean and the beaches had to be closed for periods of time. You could walk down the beach and see toilet paper at the waters edge. The old days of clean ponds and streams were replaced by new times with the oceans being polluted and people still wanted the property.

There was a job opening near my old home with

a significant increase in salary and I moved back.

Dad also sold the little Cape Cod that I was raised in and used the combined money from the two house sales to build a beautiful home on 300 ft. of lakefront property. My family finally had a home that was at least as good as the homes of my high-school friends and in most cases it was better. It didn't make much difference now because all of my high-school friends were gone from the area.

I thought that I could live at home again, but it would be impossible after having been so free. Everything was back to the old days. Dad would come home and complain that I parked the car too close to the front of the garage and he couldn't get into the closet. Imagine me being accused of keeping someone out of the closet! The next time, I parked the car further back and he complained that it was too far back and almost hit the garage door when it came down. I would actually be tense the entire time that he was home because I wondered what I would be doing wrong next. I bought a new Buick Electra Convertible with air conditioning. It was 1967 and automobile air-conditioning was starting to become popular, but I was reluctant to bring the car home because I knew my father would not approve. The assumption was correct and he found a number of faults with the car. You only use air-conditioning a couple months of the year and it is just something else to break down. Then on a hot August day, mom and dad had to go to a wedding. They got dressed in formal clothes and were suffocating from the heat. Mom suggested that they borrow my car with air conditioning and to my surprise, he agreed. They went to the wedding in my car and didn't say much about it, but bought an air-conditioned car a short time later.

Through out my college years, I took advantage of the free entertainment of Bud's racing. Moving on to a teaching job provided even more time to enjoy my access to famous people and their horses in all of the grandeur of race track, club house privileges and even some pictures in the winner's circle. It soon became obvious that one of the twins, Bart, was interested in Bud's wife. He encouraged Bud to go out with him and pick up women. Buds wife eventually realized what was going on and initially blamed Bart because she realized that he was the instigator. She threw Bud out of the house and he rented a motel room near my place of employment. I sometimes stopped there after work for cocktails and I accidentally met him at the bar one afternoon. He explained what had happened and gave me his room number so that I would call from the lobby when I came in for a drink. The phone call worked on the next few visits and we had some afternoon drinks together. One afternoon, I dialed the room and the conversation was very strange. He later explained that he had a woman in the room and couldn't talk freely while she was listening. So, the next time I came through the lobby, I dialed the room number and said, "Bud, if you don't have a whore in the sack, come on down to the cocktail lounge". The fellow that answered the phone was not too happy about my invitation and I quickly learned that Bud had moved out. A traveling guest moved in for the night. I decided that it might be best to skip cocktails that afternoon and made a fast exit.

Bud was not what I would consider good-looking and there was no sexual interest, but his life style was so exciting that I spent a great deal of time with him. He had to drive his car from one race track to another and spend many hours on the road. He loved it if I would do the driving while he slept in the back seat and I liked to drive, so it worked well for both of us. When they took a private airplane to a race, I was still invited and that was really exciting. The pilot kept asking me to fly the plane, so I took flying lessons. Bud bought a 28 ft. fishing boat and had a smaller speedboat that was docked near our beach house in the year before dad sold it. His wife loved the beach and he hated it, but we let them use our beach house and she could enjoy the ocean while he was enjoying his boats.

One night, he raced at a track near Atlantic City and we were driving back to the beach house along the beach. He wanted to stop on Long Beach Island because of an organist that was entertaining. The organist, Leroy Lewis, had an unbelievable amount of equipment and did an unbelievable show for a real party crowd. A large, three keyboard, electric organ sat in the middle of a square bar and was connected to other instruments around the room. The keyboard controlled an old honky-tonk piano, a xylophone, a glockenspiel, drums and I can't remember what else. Bud told me that Leroy was an excellent organist, but watch out for him and the group of guys at the bar behind him because they were all gay. It wasn't a gay bar, but it was the first time that I had seen a group of openly gay people and I returned by myself on the following weekend. As usual, nothing happened except that I became a regular customer and continued to return. I sat directly in front of the organ and Leroy eventually started making remarks to me. His theme song was Step to the Rear and from him it was more than a song title. He was not attractive and I was not interested in him, but could not say the same about the rest of his private following. One of them invited me to a different bar a few blocks away and I went. This was a 100 percent gay bar and a shock to me. I had never seen men dancing together or kissing each other and I was about to do it with my new host. The experience left me feeling so guilty that I stayed away from the area for a few weeks. A few weeks later, I went back to the original bar and thought that a few drinks would give me the nerve to go into the gay bar again. Much to my surprise, Bud and several neighbors from our hometown area where at a table in the bar. They called me over to their table and I joined them. Bud wanted his group to see how the entire bar would join in a line dance when Leroy played "When the Saints Go Marching In", but he requested the song three times and Leroy would not play it. I shouted the song title to Leroy and he stopped in the middle of what he was playing and switched to it. I said to myself, " oh Christ I don't believe he did that ". Nobody seemed to take notice of the special response that I received and I managed to stay in the closet for at least one more night.

My next trip to Long Beach Island was directly to the gay bar. It is impossible to explain the overwhelming feeling of excitement that gave me a rush as I parked the car in the lot. I was in my twenties and never had an opportunity to date or even cruise for somebody interesting and the building in front of me was full of good looking, partying, gay people that were not in the closet. I would be able to make a pass at anyone and not care who saw me doing it. One of the best looking guys in my hometown, Don, had me frustrated on many occasions because he was a great looking honor student from the impressive part of town, star football player, going out with the best looking girl in school and a nice person that did not have a stuck up attitude. He would be the type that I was looking for and much to my surprise; he was at the bar with two other guys. We saw each other at the same time and exchanged a wave of hands. I wondered if he was upset over the fact that I saw him, but he eventually came over and said that it was about time he met somebody from home that he could smile at and say hello the next time we pass in the post office. He excused himself and returned to his seat because he was with a date. The only thing that I could think about was the smug feeling that I would get the next time that I would see his snob girlfriend that was obviously his closet door and possibly the one who turned him to men.

This time, I went home with a customer that was staying there on Long Beach Island. He tried to teach me how to be a bottom and I quickly learned that I was not into his scene and there was a quick conclusion to that evening. That experience did not stop me from becoming a regular customer at the bar where I found a wallet on the floor during a future visit. The bartender and I looked at the wallet for identification and the driver's license indicated that the owner lived near my home. Long Beach Island was an hour's drive from my home and I now had the address of a gay bar customer who lived 10 minutes from my home. The trip to return his wallet was somewhat scary because I considered the fact that he might look like Leroy Lewis, but that would simply mean returning the wallet and walking away, so I went. He was actually nice looking and I was about to learn that I enjoy oral sex. We discussed where I found his wallet and he explained that his gay lover was a school teacher in the winter and worked at a bar on Long Beach Island as a technician for organ equipment. Small world, I was with Leroy Lewis' technician's lover who was one of those not so bad looking members of the gay crowd behind the organ. The evening ended with information about gay bars located in our immediate area and once again I was shocked to learn what was going on without me knowing about it.

Another week went by as I anxiously awaited the opportunity to discover my own neighborhood's out of the closet crowd. There were actually four gay bars in the worst parts of neighboring Trenton, but they all provided some type of security as was necessary. I became very friendly with a good looking bartender, Michael, at one of the gay bars and we started taking weekend trips to the gay beach at Atlantic City. Michael was part Indian from Oklahoma and the other part must have been Irish because he was a handsome blond that liked to drink. He certainly didn't have an inferiority complex and was very outspoken without reservation. We were both in the ocean swimming one Saturday. I came out first and stood at the waters edge. A straight woman was walking down the beach and she stopped because she saw two guys kissing in the water. She expected me to agree with her when she said, "Isn't that disgusting?" As she spoke to me, Michael came out of the water and put an arm around me. We turned and headed toward our blanket and I stopped Michael so that I could turn around and see the reaction on the woman's face.

I was aware of the fact that Michael had a sugar daddy who bought the bar for Michael and paid for his apartment. The sugar daddy also became aware of the fact that we were going to the beach together and he waited for us to return one Saturday night. Michael, his twinky, was driving my car when we pulled into the parking lot and he didn't realize that I would be on the passenger side as he knocked on my window. He simply announced that he knew what was going on and return to the bar. I received a telephone call the next day and was told that our next trip to Atlantic City would have to be canceled because daddy was taking twinky. I had been spending a lot of time at the local airport because of my horse racing friends and I had learned to fly a plane. I couldn't resist flying over the Atlantic City gay beach and waving the plane at Michael and daddy Bill. I told Michael that I was going to fly over them and I should have realized that he would tell daddy who was waving the wings of a plane over a gay beach. The next time that I went into the bar, daddy said "here comes jet pilot" and I acquired the nick name JP. It was originally an insult because the plane was a single engine Piper Cherokee, but most people didn't know the origin and everybody called me J.P.

I never went out with the bartender again and we all became good friends. Daddy Bill was a local lawyer whose real name was Seymour. He was always funny and I enjoyed hearing his jokes, but Michael could keep the rest at the cost of sleeping with Bill. Michael was an alcoholic with little self control and he needed a lawyer sugar daddy to keep him out of jail. Michael got drunk and mistakenly drove over a bridge to Pennsylvania without any money for the toll. He told a state trooper that he didn't want to cross the fucking bridge anyway and got arrested for hitting the trooper. Daddy told me the story and said that Michael cannot drink. It was interesting to realize that daddy bought him a bar and said that he could not drink. A few weeks later, Michael was drunk in another bar that I visited and I saw him getting into problems with the owner. I called daddy Bill, who lived with his mother, to let him know before the problem got serious. Bill's mother shouted to Bill, "It's for you and it's one of your fag friends because he said Bill, not Seymour." Well, I already knew I was a fag and was now acknowledged as somebody's friend too. Bill got Michael on the phone and was able to control him, which amazed me. Bill seemed like he was very healthy, but he went into the hospital and we never knew why. He died in the hospital and nobody ever knew the cause of death. AIDS was not discovered at that time, but he may have been one of the early victims during the time when they were starting to discover cases and unaware of the disease. Michael wasn't his only interest. He enjoyed going to a truck stop on Route 1 to meet truck drivers. He had two partners in a law business. They were trying to push him out of the business because they found out that he owned a gay bar. It was sort of like a soap opera where I missed the last episode. Truck stops, bathhouses, and adult bookstores were the extremes of gay promiscuity.   I was in an adult bookstore near McGuire Air Force Base when the clerk answered a telephone call. He hung up the phone and started to laugh. He couldn't resist telling me that the person on the phone had just asked him to check video booth #9 and see if there was a set of false teeth on the

seat. Some old bird got so excited that he forgot
to put his teeth back in.

Chapter 11 - Building a Church

It wasn't the 1940's anymore and there were
some changes in social life. I saw my first mall in
Florida and thought that it would be much more
beneficial in New Jersey where you needed to
escape the winter weather as you walked from
store to store. They appeared in New Jersey and
became places for social gathering as well as
shopping. Everyone had television with 13
channels. Schools remained to be a source of
many activities, but they were more structured
and took on some aspects of a serious business
with many demands on the participants.
Churches had to compete for a place in this
society of diversified offerings and busy
schedules. Mom made sure that our family
stayed involved in the church to the extent that I
had become president of a church board of
trustees.

The church was a beautiful old building in the
center of town. The membership wanted to add
recreational facilities and air conditioning. The
design of the church made it impractical to add
air-conditioning and the center city location
eliminated any possibility of adding recreational
facilities. Parking was another major problem in
that location.   A 3:00 a.m. telephone call
awakened me with information that the church
was on fire. Fortunately, we never considered
the idea of relocation or I might have been

accused of setting the fire. I didn't think so at the time, but I was actually just a young kid in my early 20s and this church was giving me some major responsibilities. On two different occasions, the last surviving member of wealthy farmer families had died and left their entire estate to the church. I opened the barn door at one of the farms and found a Model A Ford in perfect condition. It was a major task to auction off the personal property, sell the real estate and invest the proceeds. There were a number of wealthy members in the church and we never had difficulty raising money. The fire had done significant damage to the church and the local insurance company offered a large settlement. Half of the congregation wanted to restore the old facility because of items like the stained glass windows which were donated in memory of family members. Others wanted to take this opportunity and relocate to a new and more functional facility. This created an even greater problem for me as president of the church board. We finally resolved the problem by agreeing to use historical items from the old church in our construction of a new facility. There were eight stained-glass windows that suffered damage from the heat of the fire. At a cost of $25,000 each, the stained-glass pieces were removed from the original lead and reassembled for installation in the new building.

There were some advantages to working with a church and also some disadvantages. I could call on free legal advice from attorneys that were members of the church and it was easy to negotiate excellent contracts. When the architect informed me that the builder was behind schedule, a short telephone call to our attorneys resolved the problem. The contracts required that the builder be bonded and there was a completion date with a penalty clause. Our attorney's telephone call to the bonding company was enough to get us back on schedule. Problems came from the fact that there were too many people to keep satisfied. The building committee would select colors schemes, furniture and interior designs after numerous arguments. Then they would mutually agree that they did not like what they had chosen after seeing it in a finished state. We rebuilt the minister's podium three times in a variety of square and oval shapes.

The finished church was a centrally air-conditioned building with recreational facilities, a dining hall that even included a commercial dishwasher, and 3 acres of parking. It was very functional and opened without a mortgage. The large brick structure had beautiful stained-glass windows to satisfy a few members of the church. Another major contributor was pleased that we answered his request for laminated arches supporting natural wood beams in the ceiling. A church furniture Co. was brought in from Lancaster Pennsylvania to design church pews that matched the interior wood and had cushioned seats for some of the elderly ladies. We even satisfied requests for restrooms in specified areas. I have to pat myself on the back and say that it was a remarkable feat for what I would now consider a young kid.

I did receive one immediate benefit from the project. The local Cadillac dealer was on the building committee. He and I made several trips to building material suppliers and subcontractors. I usually drove my Chrysler car and we always stopped at his Cadillac dealership when we passed the location. One day, we pulled up to the front door of the Cadillac dealership and went inside to see his son who was running the business. He told his son to sell me a Cadillac regardless of how much they had to lose on the deal because he could not continue coming to his own dealership in a Chrysler. I bought my first Cadillac and was the only teacher that had one in the school parking lot. My route to school went past a donut store. The cafeteria manager asked me to stop and pick up donuts for the cafeteria. I drove around to the cafeteria loading dock and parked next to a bread delivery truck that was falling apart. As the driver opened his door, it almost fell off of the truck. I opened my trunk and took donuts out of my Cadillac. He looked at me and the donuts coming from a Cadillac with a pathetic face and very seriously said, "There must be more money in donuts than bread." It made me laugh for the rest of the day.

My father's oldest brother visited him one weekend. The three brothers seldom saw each other because the oldest was living in Pennsylvania, dad was in New Jersey, and the youngest was in Long Island. I was there with my new Cadillac and we all decided to take a Cadillac ride to the youngest brother's home in Long Island. Our little day trip took us past the cemetery where grand pop was buried. Grand Mom had died during my senior year in college and was buried with grand pop. Believe it or not, her undertaker's name was really "Willdig". Dad wanted to stop at his father and mother's grave. He really shocked me that day. This man had never shown an emotional moment in my entire life. Weeds were growing around the gravestone and dad said that it looked terrible. He started crying and said, "I'll take care of it pop ". Then he got down on his hands and knees and crawled around the grave pulling weeds. It almost made me cry to have seen this stone hard person find something that reduced him to crying and crawling on his knees. I couldn't help but notice that he never said a word about his mother in the same grave. It was difficult to understand how a man that was so close to his own father was so removed from his son.

Chapter 12 - Opportunities Knocked at my Door

Computers were emerging in our society, but they had not entered the business office or the instructional programs of the public high-school. A Federal program offered pilot funds to high-schools that would embark on an instructional program in computers. I was one of the few teachers in our school district that had taken computer courses in college and I volunteered to set up a program for acquiring the federal funds. As with most federally funded programs, it was a waste of money. They provided out of date IBM punch card equipment that was already phased out. I managed to bring the program up to date by acquiring a leased line to the local county college computer system. It was an extremely awkward situation because we only had one terminal connected to the computer. Students wrote programs on paper and I provided what should be on-line syntax checking. When a program was finally completed on paper, the student would be allowed to type it into the system and see the results.

At the same time, the teachers' association requested an additional deduction field on their payroll. The old Burroughs accounting machine that was being used by the business office, could not handle an additional column for another deduction field. I was on the salary negotiating team for the teachers' association and had already entered all of the teachers' contract information into the county computer so that we could project the total cost of proposed salary guides. When the Board of Education saw our total reports from the computer, they started submitting salary guides for total cost analysis of their own proposals. The board could no longer complete the payroll on their Boroughs accounting machine, so they ask me to create a program to do payroll on the county computer. It had previously taken the board office three days to complete the payroll using the Borough's ledger sheets and manually inserted checks.

Each employee's year to date totals from the previous line of data was keyed in for the current pay calculation and followed by entry of data for the current pay period. The computer stored all of the contract information and year-to-date totals. Completing a payroll on the computer was reduced to the simple task of entering hours for hourly employees. It took approximately 15 minutes to complete the payroll on a computer rather than three days of typing ledger sheets and checks. Consequently, I was told that my class load would be reduced to three glasses per day if I would put the entire school budget on the computer. I was reluctant to do this because we were dependent on the county college and limited in our access to their computer. The school district was paying significant amounts for outside companies to complete student scheduling, school bus scheduling and other services. I suggested that we bring these functions into house and use moneys allocated for those services to purchase our own computer system. The idea was approved and our little high school was one of the first schools to offer a real program of computer study in addition to having a computerized board office without increasing our budget for the purchase.

It was an amazing thing for the school district. We had a classroom with 20 computer terminals. Under the old system, each department within the school submitted budget requests. The requests were combined to create ledger sheet totals for each category of expenditure. When the ledger sheets indicated that a category had expended its budgeted amount, future purchases were turned down for that item. It usually meant that if somebody else got to your budgeted amount first, you lost it. The new computerized system charged each purchase to a department and maintained a record of remaining funds available to that department. At the end of September, the first of monthly statements were sent to each department showing how much they had spent and what was still available. This met with great approval. The school librarian said that for the first time, she would be able to purchase a book in June by keeping a reserve for new publications. Of course, we had a few of the usual growing pains that come with anything new and especially with computers. A parent attended one of our board of education meetings and waited for us to open the floor to comments from visitors. He stood up and held an envelope high in his right hand. He seemed to enjoy pointing out the fact that the computer had sent a 12¢ library fine to his home in an envelope having a 25¢ stamp on it. He was really enjoying the fact that we had done something dumb and his analysis was exactly accurate. If he hadn't been so arrogant, I would have laughed and agreed with him, but his attitude made me do a reverse attack. I told him that this was an educational institution and not a business run for profit. We didn't mind spending 13¢ to teach our students a lesson in responsibility. After having waited two hours for his great moment, it was shot down in less than a minute. On another occasion, we had replaced the cheerleading coach with a substitute during her maternity leave. The substitute reported that one of the cheerleaders lost her uniform, but she wasn't aware of the cost and left the amount field empty. A few days later, I received a telephone call from a parent because our computer had sent a letter requesting payment of zero for the zero balance owed. The letter went on to say that the amount may seem insignificant, but the total of insignificant amounts becomes a valid concern. He indicated that sending a check for zero would not be a problem if that was what we wanted. This time, we both had a good laugh over the ridiculous letter. The most memorable experience came from our girl's physical education teacher. She taught a course called Family Living where in students were paired off as couples and had to prepare budgets for a mock family. She had a personality inventory questionnaire for matching couples and asked if they could be run through the computer for matching the couples. I told her that it would be okay, but number the sheets rather than using names so that the confidential information could be keyed into the computer by students. She stopped in the office and picked up the results that showed which numbers were matched to other numbers and headed for the classroom. A few minutes later, she returned to my office in laughter. She told me that we forgot something. We should have made a blue pile and a pink pile because the computer matched the captain of the football team with the gayest little sissy boy in the school. Fortunately, she realized the mistake before reading it out loud. From my viewpoint, it wasn't all that much of a mistake, but I had to treat it as a mistake. Many clergymen and hopeful parents are of the opinion that a gay guy will change his mind if he will just try a night with a nice girl. They would be surprised to learn that gay men have a tendency to think that any straight man would become gay if he tried a good man. There is a gay saying, "Ditch the Bitch and Switch".

The close of each marking period had formerly been a major problem. Report cards were typed for each student and placed in metal trays by home room assignment. Preparing the trays was a week long, guidance department task. The following week involved teachers spending many hours in the staff work room to locate their students' report cards and enter grades manually. It was a nightmare for teachers because there was a constant wait for the availability of your next homeroom tray to record a single student's grade. The lengthy process meant that report cards were usually distributed a few weeks after the close of the marking period. The new computerized system produced grade sheets by class for each teacher. They could be completed in less than an hour at home or anywhere. When they were returned to the front office, a secretary would enter the course number into a computer terminal and the student names for that class would appear. In a few seconds, the 25 or 30 grades could be entered next to the appropriate student names. Finally, the computer would take an hour to produce an easy to read and impressive report card for each student sorted by homeroom. Report cards could be distributed three days after the close of the marking period rather than three weeks after the close of the marking period.

We did encounter a few problems with the report card program. The guidance department had to use abbreviated names for courses with long names. They entered the Introductory Analysis course name as Intro Analysis. The computer could only fit 10 letters in the courses title area of the report cards. Count out 10 letters and see what you get. Once again, I received a phone call from a parent. Fortunately, this mother had a good sense of humor. She said that it was normally her pleasure to see her son get an "A" grade, but she would have preferred that he receive a failing grade in Intro Anal. The computer listed all of the students with honor society grades of B or higher. A list was sent to the local newspaper for publication. It needed some human intervention because one of our special education students had high grades in his classes for slow learners. The town was not happy about their school claiming that a kid who could not tie his own shoes was an honor student in their community.

Supply requisitions, minimum inventory purchase orders, student fine billings, honor student reports and an unending list of projects were computerized.

New Jersey required school districts to submit a detailed record of student attendance on an approved state form. Most school districts employed one person to spend the entire day making the detailed entries in a state attendance register. Our attendance clerk hated the computer because it did her job in a few minutes and put the daily absence sheet in the teachers' hands before the end of the first period. A neighboring school district had purchased an automated system to record their attendance. Their new system did not work and they could not produce the required reports at the end of the second month of school. State financial assistance was based on attendance records and had to be withheld in their absence. Each School District had a Board of Education Secretary that was in a state wide association of board secretaries. Secretary was a somewhat misleading title because they actually functioned like the corporate executive officer of a company. Our board secretary, Florence K., told the neighboring school about our efficient system. They asked me to visit them to discuss their problem. People smoked almost everywhere in those days and the administration offices were in a separate office building. I entered with a cigarette in my hand and the superintendent of school's secretary was nasty about my coming in with a cigarette. If her comment had been a request rather than an insult, I would have thrown the cigarette out side. She had me so annoyed that I decided this was not a place that I wanted to assist. I told her to inform the superintendent of schools that I showed up for my appointment, but since I was not allowed in the office because I smoked, the meeting would have to be canceled. The Board Secretary, Hoby

S., heard the conversation and came out of his office. He told her to find an ash tray somewhere and bring it into the conference room where we would be meeting. Knowing that she could hear me, I told Hoby that he could get rid of the ashtray because it really wasn't that important, but if I was going to be returning, I might ask him to get rid of that nasty secretary too, because her attitude is much more negative than my cigarettes. This was a great moment for someone who had suffered from an inferiority complex. The nasty old bitch was at her desk wondering if her mouth had jeopardized her employment. School districts were all nonprofit organizations that cooperated with each other and there was no doubt that I could offer our computer to produce their state attendance records while they waited for hardware installation. One of their school secretaries came to my school and enter there absenteeism into our computer. Within a few days, their state attendance registers were printed and they started receiving state funds. They were so pleased with the system that they wanted to have all of the programs being used in my school. I had almost walked away from this school district which was going to make my own school realize the value of my services. The new school would liked to have had me on their staff and Florence K was aware of it.

I have to be very grateful to Florence for having taught me everything she knew about school business administration laws and procedures. Although Florence was an advocate of our computer, she warned me that she was a computer nerd. The first time that she tried to run a payroll, the computer stopped because it would not print a negative check. The program indicated that the rate of pension deduction be entered as a decimal and she entered 5 where it should have been .05. The resulting calculation took 5 times the employees pay as a deduction for pension and resulted in a negative net pay. I changed to program so that it would beep for any entry that seemed wrong. It was funny to hear her work at the computer because it sounded like somebody was sending Morse code, but she did get the job done. She was near the age of retirement and encouraged me to take the necessary courses for moving into her job. The courses were very easy because I had learned more from Florence and my own projects for the school than they taught in the courses. There were times when the professor made notes from my remarks for use in his future lectures. He knew the requirements and functions of a board secretary, but never experienced some of the problems that can happen. Our gasoline pump was used by the bus drivers, driver's education teachers, maintenance staff and administrators. There was a system for recording the use of gasoline, but we never considered it necessary to enforce our system. I do not think that there was any unauthorized use of the gasoline, but people do not complete paperwork as they should. Florence was closing the books one year and told me that she didn't know what to do about the gasoline. She continued to say that she needed to charge 10,000 gallons of gasoline to evaporation and spillage. It wasn't really funny, but we were laughing at the ridiculous situation and Florence's solution. From that time forward, a maintenance man was assigned to verify the total usage on the pump meter each day.

There were many times when direct involvement made me more knowledgeable about running the schools than the state department of education. The state mandated a minimum basic skills test. School districts were directed to place failing students in special instruction classes of 6 or fewer students. I knew that the failing students were the students that never came to school. It resulted in our assigning teachers to classrooms that would be empty every day and we were paying a teacher to check the empty room before going to the staff room. The staff gave me a standing ovation when I attended a meeting and suggested that we could improve the New Jersey schools by placing a bomb under the state department of education in Trenton and blow it across the Delaware River to Pennsylvania where it could screw up Pennsylvania instead of New Jersey. When we tried to resolve attendance problems, we found that we had nothing to use for enforcement under the existing laws. Our truant officer went to a girls home when he noticed that both a girlfriend and boyfriend were absent. The boyfriend answered the door at the girl's house and he was standing there in his underwear. The truant officer said that he could see what was going on and the boy said, 'Don't knock it until you try it". Our truant officer decided that he couldn't argue with that statement. She signed up for summer school to finish classes that she failed because of poor attendance. Our secretary called her home when she was absent from summer school the third time. Her father said that she must be pregnant because she throws up every morning. Her boyfriend told the truant officer that he shouldn't knock it, but it was the boyfriend that shouldn't have knocked it because he knocked her up. The boyfriend wore jeans when he wasn't down to his underwear, so it was easy for me to understand why the girlfriend got into trouble.

There was a state wide movement against New Jersey's system of local real-estate taxes supporting individual school districts because wealthy neighborhoods provided better funding to upset the balance of equality in available education across the various school districts. Consequently, the state required a new system of cost accounting called program oriented budgeting. The idea was to determine exactly how much was being spent per capita for each area of instruction. The program met with great opposition because the school districts were not capable of doing this on their existing ledger sheet systems. We were already doing it on our computer and were very happy with the results. I was asked to speak to a number of superintendents of schools because we were advocating the many advantages of an efficient accounting system. After the meeting, several school districts asked for my assistance and our software was soon to be shared by 18 different school districts. Most people that needed a restroom in their travels would stop at a gas station, but I had master keys to every school in the area and would look for a school.

I was completely removed from all classroom assignments and shared by two schools as coordinator of computer services while contracting with numerous other schools for software. The average school teacher contract was $12,500 per year and I was suddenly making $75,000 per year for a shared agreement between two schools plus several $10,000 contracts from other schools. I installed foreign exchange lines in my home to control computers outside of our local calling district. You could pick up a phone in the kitchen and call a foreign exchange number which could be answered in the bedroom as a toll call. It became my favorite line to say that my house was so big that it was a toll call from the kitchen to the bedroom.

My official title was coordinator of computer services. The split contracts eliminated disclosure of my in come to any individual school and nobody knew that I was making more than the superintendent of schools.

It became traditional for me to throw a closing day party for the school staff each June. My home had a large swimming pool, volleyball court, horseshoes and an outdoor sound system. One of the teachers told me that I didn't live like a teacher. Some of the nice looking men on staff gave me reason to suspect that they might be gay, but I was never really sure. One of them arrived early and changed into his bathing suit while talking to me in my dining room. It was almost as though he wanted to expose himself because he knew where my house had two bathrooms, three bedrooms, a private office and a secluded den. The physical education teacher would usually stay after the party and lay on the den floor watching television with me. He wore the boxer type bathing suits with an inner lining which always seemed to be hanging out of one leg. He had previously been in my office at school and sat on the corner of my desk in black spandex shorts and made it obvious that he was a big guy, in every respect. The janitors put chains on most of the schools exterior doors at about 4:00. If I stayed beyond 4:00 p.m., I had to exit through the boy's locker room where he would frequently be in the shower. I did see the naked football team at their lockers, but was careful not to take a good look at them or the shower.

We had purchased our computer from a very handsome, single salesman named James. Each time a school district asked for my software, I sent them to James for a computer. He was making so much money on computer sales that he opened his own business. A classroom full of computer terminals and a business office with high speed printers would cost between $30,000 and $100,000. I was working with 18 school districts and it made a nice little business for James. Each buyer would subsequently get service contracts that ranged from $200 to

$2,000 per month. Needless to say, we became very friendly and frequently stopped at my local hotel bar for an end of the day drink. I made it a point to know the bartender because he looked like Patrick Swayze and wore tailored clothes that fit like a glove. He was there when Bud stayed at the motel and knew both of us. Work had kept me busy and the race tracks were not drawing the old betting crowd subsequent to legalized off track betting. I wasn't going to the track and had not been going out with Bud for some time. Our bartender told me that Bud's wife married Bart. It was hard for me to believe that she married the man that caused her husband to cheat, but life can be strange. Bud died of a heart attack a few years later, but his wife, Bart, and Bart's ex-wife are all good friends now.

One day, James came into my office and said that he was going to Philadelphia to deliver a computer terminal and wanted to know if I would go with him. Philadelphia was my home away from home because I had been going out with a Philadelphia guy named Frank. James didn't realize that I was gay and my sexual attraction to him had worn off after spending so much time with him, but I knew that our friendship was strong enough to endure almost anything. He made his delivery and I took him to a gay bar in the early afternoon. There were no customers because of the early hour and we sat down for drinks. A Philadelphia judge came in and sat next to James. They introduce themselves to each other and everything was fine at first. Then the judge bought James a drink and started making passes at him. James told me that he wanted to leave after this drink and we were soon outside. He said, "That's a gay bar isn't it" Then he went around to the side of the building to pee because he had been afraid to use the men's room in the bar. I wasn't going to deny anything, but he still assumed that I was straight and that this was just a joke I was playing on him.

The National Education Association chartered flights to Europe and sold seats at ridiculously low prices. I decided to spend a summer in Europe and did something that I would never do today. I flew to Paris without any reservations or plans other than to wander around Europe all summer. Mom's youngest brother, Uncle Tom, was stationed in Bremen Germany, so I took a train to his apartment and knocked on the door. His wife opened the door and said "Jesus Christ, Tom, you are never going to believe who is standing in the door ". I stayed with them for a couple of weeks and enjoyed a taste of life in Germany. Tom drove us down to spend two days in Amsterdam and tour the city on their canal boats. I had to see the famous dikes of Amsterdam. They were not what I expected. The old stories about a boy sticking his finger in the dike made me think of something more like a dam. It was a surprise to see a big earthen mound that was more like an isthmus or a long jetty with a highway on top. It was too wide and high for you to see the water on both sides without walking from side to side and I didn't get the feeling that I was on a dike. Every few miles, there were control gates that were like a concrete dam with large steel sections that could be raised to allow water flow through the dike. It was an education for me and I should have deducted the cost of the trip from my income tax as an educational expense for a teacher.

I bought hundreds of souvenirs and gifts which Tom could send back to the United States via the military mail service. Germany impressed me as one of the cleanest countries that I had ever seen and many of the people spoke better English than I would hear at home. Amsterdam, which I had always heard was so clean, actually had litter and beverage cans in the gutters, just like home. Museums had never interested me in the United States, but I spent many days in the Paris Louvre. I did look at the famous Mona Lisa picture and was not impressed by that. The Egyptian displays were my favorite. The Paris subway system was very easy to use and took me all over the city. There were so many things to see that I could have stayed for another month. Notre Dame Cathedral, many palaces, Great River cruises, the Eiffel Tower, sidewalk cafes, the opera house, Arch D' Triumph, Champs Elyse, and more.

Writing computer programs has always been more like a hobby than work for me. I did not mind returning to work after by summer in Europe. The schools were happy with the services that they were receiving and I had nice offices in many of them. Nobody knew where or when I was working and it wasn't like having a 9 to 5 job. It was my preferred way of working because I could be productive and see the immediate results of my productivity. They actually got more than their money's worth because I enjoyed my work and never refused to do anything. I programmed their bell systems to ring in the correct areas at designated times for class changes. I programmed their telephone systems to designate the calling restrictions for each extension. I even selected their banking institutions because we interfaced our computers for automatic bank reconciliation and money transfers. School districts received their $10 million budgets from quarterly tax revenues and held significant deposits in banks. Participating in the selection of these banks gave me some real privileges. My regular routine involved depositing funds collected by student activity programs. I could go to the bank after they closed their teller windows at 2:00 p.m. and they would reopen a window for me. My grandmother was living near me and her health was failing. She gave me a power of attorney that authorized me to control her bank accounts. I stopped at a branch office near my grandmother's home to withdraw some cash for her. The drive-through teller was being extremely difficult. She was insisting that I drive to the main office where the power of attorney was on file. The main office was 20 miles away and I was only withdrawing $20. It would have cost me $10 to drive my big Cadillac to the main office and back. I told her to call the main office and tell them that I was at her drive-through window and becoming very annoyed. Within a few minutes, there was a change in her manner and $20 in her drive-through drawer.

I felt like I had used my banking leverage to do something for my grandmother and enjoyed telling her about the incident. Although I couldn't do anything wrong in her eyes, it was always rewarding to do something right because she was so appreciative. She went into the local hospital at age 86. The hospital called and asked me to come sign papers. I met with my grandmother and her doctor who wanted to remove a tumor. Grandmom did not want the operation and her doctor wanted me to sign the permission form. I told the doctor that my grandmother was not senile and it would be her decision. Grandmom looked the doctor straight in the eyes and sternly asked, "Did you hear what he said?" It was the right decision because she lived for a considerable time longer and eventually died of a heart attack unrelated to her stomach tumor. She probably would have had the heart attack from an operation at her age.

Chapter 13 - Discovering Other Gays

These were the best years of my life. I was a sexually desirable young male with money to spend. Times were changing and I was discovering the availability of other gay men that were attractive.

I could not afford the spring break trips to Fort Lauderdale when I was in college. With movies like, " Where The Boys Are ", I was definitely going to be at the next spring break in Fort Lauderdale.

Mom and Dad took their first trip to Florida when a developer offered free accommodations in return for visiting their Florida sales presentation. They both enjoyed Fort Lauderdale and had been returning in the previous few years. They told me how nice it was on the Fort Lauderdale beach while I weathered the New Jersey snow and they added to my desire for a Florida vacation.

My first few trips were to a small motel on the beach that was managed by two elderly women. It was so great to enjoy swimming in April with warmer ocean temperatures than we ever saw in New Jersey, that I didn't look for any gay activity. I did enjoy watching the straight guys and bought a camera with a telephoto lens. Four college boys parked a van by the bathroom window of my motel room. I watched them leave the van and head for the beach until they were out of sight. They returned with one girl after half an hour. She went into the van with those four hot guys and I tried to imagine the great time that she must be having.   Six college guys rented a suite next to my motel room and I got friendly with one of them.   He spent many hours in the pool with a girl that must have been about 15 years old. She was vacationing with her family and I was surprised that they allowed her to spend so much time with a college guy. Not only was he older than her, but he wore a white bathing suit that should have had something underneath. You could even see is black crotch hair through his white bathing suit. One morning, he told me that he finally nailed her on the rooftop sundeck the previous night. He really made me feel like I was missing something in life because society didn't permit me to have what this 15 year-old girl achieved. The incident encouraged me to walk down the beach a few blocks and go into the gay Marlin Beach Hotel. It was an early afternoon and there were only a few customers at the bar. I met a physical education teacher from Michigan named Troy. Straight physical education teacher seems to be an oxymoron. His body made it obvious that he was a physical education teacher and I was enjoying thoughts about what might happen. Neither of us was forward enough to make the first move even though we were in a gay bar. He gave me his Michigan address and phone number. It was my turn to take the next step, but I did not know how. He had a sunburn and said that he needed to take a shower and get the salt water off of his skin. Now that he had almost asked for an invitation to my room, I said that my motel room was only a few blocks away and he could take a shower if he wanted. We went to my room where he stripped naked and talked to me for a long time before going into the shower. I wanted to see the naked bodies of the four guys in the van and my neighbor with his white bathing suit. Seeing the naked physical education teacher was actually more than I expected and somewhat satisfied my anxieties. He came out of the shower and laid face down on the bed. Neither of us admitted that we were gay, but he proceeded to say that when he was horny, he could fuck anything. It was my turn again and there wasn't much more that he could say in the way of an invitation. The entire scene was so new to me that I never took the next step and was satisfied to have seen him naked. I changed my mind a few months later and wrote a few letters to him in Michigan. He must have given up on me because he never answered my letters.

A guy came over to my blanket on a straight beach in New Jersey. I assumed that he was not gay because we were on a straight beach. My first reaction was reluctance to make small talk with someone that I did not know and I was annoyed by his approach. His excuse for talking to me was in a magazine that I had lying on my blanket. He told me that he had done an advertisement and his picture was in the magazine. This got my interest and sure enough his picture was in the magazine. He invited me to spend a weekend in Philadelphia, where I discovered a whole new world of gay people. This was an unbelievable experience because they occupied an entire area of that large city. There were at least 20 bars, restaurants, parks, and even the grocery stores were gay. It was also the first time that I realized how most gay people were much better at keeping beautiful homes. Their showplaces exceeded the fine homes of wealthy people in my hometown. When you stand in a club with 500 other gay people, you get the first time experience of believing that there is nothing unusual about being gay. My host, Frank, had a beautiful, two-story town house, with a loft bedroom in Center City Philadelphia. We sat by his fireplace in the living room and listened to Diana Ross sing Touch Me In The Morning and eventually moved to the loft bedroom. Those old LP record players would play the last record over and over. Diana Ross played until the next morning and I still remember all the words to the songs on that album. Sometimes I play Diana Ross for a reminiscent return to that great night. Frank was an actor and some of his work appeared on television. His success eventually led to drug abuse and I later learned that he was found dead in a Philadelphia street gutter. The news brought tears to my eyes because I visited Frank several times and was very fond of him.

I was constantly looking for my gay bar encounter, local football player, Don, in the post office and saw his girlfriend instead. I actually felt sorry for this girl that I had envied in the past. A few weeks later, I saw Don in the local gas station and told him that I met the wrong half of an interesting couple in the post office. We both started to laugh and the attendant thought we were crazy. He told me that I was three months too late for seeing an interesting couple and one at a time was all I would get. The attendant finished his car and went to the back of mine. I had a Cadillac with a 475 engine and he always told me to turn it off so that the gas pump could catch up. After his standard joke, I walked over to the other car and said that one time with one at a time sounded like fun. He said that he wanted to spend a couple of days at the beach again and if I could stretch it to two times with one at a time, he could tell everybody that he has to excuse himself because he has a date. I was reluctant to say that we should go in one car because that means you are stuck with each other, but he said that we should go in one car. I thought, let's use the plane and leave now, but I withheld that comment and made plans for the weekend auto trip. It was a really great weekend. My attraction was mostly physical and spending the weekend together allowed me to satisfy that attraction. We stayed friendly for some time and talked about going out together again, but our paths separated before we had our second outing.

There was another gay bar in nearby Trenton called the Zodiac. A sister and brother, Patty and Jimmy, owned the bar. Jimmy was gay and their reason for having the bar. Patty's husband was a builder and his remodeling made the bar very nice. He helped the scenery by working in a T-shirt over his great body. He looked good, but that was his only attribute. He had a terrible temper and frequently beat Patty. One night, he was driving through Trenton and got into a road rage argument. The other driver shot and killed him. My response was a feeling of mixed emotions. It seemed like a waste to have lost such a great looking man, but a relief to have lost such a bastard. I went into the Zodiac bar one night and saw the brother, Harry, of one of my mother's not so conservative girl friends. He was

25 years older than me and really in the closet
with a wife and 3 children. We looked directly at
each other and there was no way for him to
avoid me. He said that if there had been a knot
hole in the floor, he would have crawled into it. I
told him that my being there meant that he could
be there and he relaxed. Sometime later, my
mother told me that Harry left his wife Helen
and ran off with his secretary. Mom was only
half correct. Harry left his wife Helen and ran
off with an Episcopal Priest, but I didn't offer
that information. On another evening at the
Zodiac, a cute young guy came over to me and
called me by name. I didn't recognize him and
he explained that he was a graduate of the school
where I worked. There were 1,200 students each
year and I didn't know all of them, but they
would know me as an administrator. He said
that he always admired me when we passed in
the halls of the school. Good old mom and dad
were spending a lot of time in Florida and their
New Jersey house was frequently empty. It was
empty that night and I made up for the fact that
I never acknowledged one of the high school
students.

I remember my favorite sign that was painted on
the men's room door at the Zodiac. "GAY
MEN'S ROOM, TRESPASSERS WILL BE
VIOLATED".

Another Trenton gay bar was the Casa Lido. A
center city area that was once a nice shopping
district was turning into a ghetto as suburban
shopping centers were causing the businesses to

fail. The Casa Lido was a converted, two story, Learner's clothing store that I previously knew from shopping with my mother. It was a long room with a double stairway at the back going up to second floor balconies. You could stand on the balconies around the outside edge of the second floor and look down through the open center to see the bar activity below. I became very friendly with a bartender named Ed and returned to the bar many times.

Chapter - 14 Alan

Daddy Bill introduced me to another of his bar customers, named Frank. I thought that he was pretty hot and continued to talk to him on future visits to the bar. One night he had a younger friend, Alan, with him and they were headed to Asbury Park. They invited me to join them and I went. My interest was really in Frank, but Alan was nice too. Little did I know that Alan lost all interest in Frank because of me. Alan came to the bar without Frank and sat with me on a subsequent night. My parents were vacationing in Florida again and I invited Alan to my home. He stayed for three days and we continued to see each other. We had talked about moving in together on a few occasions. I got into a heated battle with my father and rented an apartment to get out of his house. I took Alan to see the apartment without telling him that I had already rented it, but I had left my sunglasses on the counter and Alan was always very observing. He took one look at my sunglasses on the counter and said you already rented this didn't you. It was a large and upscale apartment in an attractive neighborhood and we moved in together. Alan's mother always had dishes drying in a rack on her kitchen counter. One fagot characteristic that I definitely have is being a neat freak. A toaster on the kitchen counter annoys me. Alan made an immediate trip to the store for a wire dish rack and rubber drain tray just like his mom's. This was the last time that I ever rented or bought a home without the stipulation that it must have a dishwasher. We were not even allowed to have our own portable dishwasher in that big apartment with ample space for one. I looked at the wire rack for two weeks and finally got into my car to fix that problem. The local appliance store must have thought that I was crazy because I said that I would buy a portable dishwasher if they could get it into the backseat of my car with the roof down. Other customers were certain that I was crazy as I parked my car at the store entrance and put the roof down in a winter snowstorm. Our unauthorized dishwasher was installed under the cover of darkness and it was the first example of how Alan and I would resolve arguments without even having the argument.

The connection to my parents was completely severed and they had no idea where I was living. A long time went by before we talked to my parents and the separation was exactly what we needed to clarify the fact that I was going to live my own life.   At least a year passed before I felt that my point was made and it would be okay to give them my phone number.

Alan and I started going to a gay beach in Belmar New Jersey. It was a beautiful town and the closest beach to our home. Unlike many of the oceanfront towns with little vacation cottages, Belmar had big mansions with wraparound porches, beautiful big yards and tree shaded streets. The residents clustered around five or six blocks of beach area in the center of town. The next few blocks to the north were usually empty and then there were four blocks of gay beach. The entire crowd would leave the beaches at about 4:00 and travel a few miles north to Asbury Park. Afternoons started at Archie's beer garden which had an outdoor patio in the sand and was perfect for the bathing suit crowd. We continued to enjoy the 4 evening bars in Asbury, but were usually too tired for that after a day on the beach and Archie's beer garden.

Asbury Park had a large gay bar with a variety of rooms. The first bar as you entered was a long room without entertainment and conducive to drinks and conversation. The next area had disco music and a large dance floor. A stairway from the inner bar went up to a lesbian bar on the second floor. Alan and I were sitting at the conversation bar and the girls' physical education teacher from my school, walked by me without saying anything. I wanted to follow her upstairs and say something to her, but Alan told me to leave her alone. The temptation was too much and I eventually went upstairs. She was sitting at a roundtable with a bunch of girls and didn't notice me. I came up behind her and tapped her on the shoulder. She looked up at me and said, I hope you're here because you're gay. I started to laugh and she was relieved to know that she was not in trouble with someone from the administration office. She did eventually get into trouble, but I had nothing to do with it. A number of parents showed up at one of our board of education meetings. The first parent to speak, requested that we install shower curtains in the girls' locker room. This was no problem and easy to accommodate. The second parent said that she didn't feel it was necessary for the girl's physical education teacher to touch the girls during supervision of the shower room. Now we knew the reason for these parents to show up at a board meeting. We simply said that this was obviously an awkward conversation for everybody at an open board meeting and could be handled better at a meeting in the office of the Superintendent of Schools. It wouldn't be possible today, but we were able to establish some guidelines for the girls' locker room that didn't include termination of the teacher.

One of the students from the school, whom I did know, graduated and eventually became a music teacher. He played the piano in one of the Asbury Park gay bars and was frequently on the beach. Wayne, was obviously not in the closet and usually entertained everyone. One afternoon on the beach, he noticed that there were dozens of ghetto blasters playing different stations. He went around to everyone and set all of the radios to the same station at a high volume to make the world's largest stereo. Then he grabbed something that looked like a microphone and did a drag show on the open beach. As usual, Wayne was unbelievably funny and gave everyone quite a show.

Atlantic City was a much longer ride, but we also went there because it had much more activity in the beach area. Most of the beach crowd would walk to the Chester Inn after swimming. They announced a hot buns contest one afternoon and I wasn't surprised to see Alan sitting on a swing. They couldn't get me up there for a thousand dollars a minute and they couldn't keep Alan away with an electric fence. If it is true that opposites attract, we were definitely meant for each other. We had an unusual degree of trust in each other and mutually agreed that having a lover doesn't exclude your appreciation for other hot guys. We fooled around with other guys while we were lovers because the one time encounters were the quickest way to end your desires for someone. Unfortunately, the guys that Alan picked were usually interested in me and the ones that I picked would usually want Alan. It was unbelievable how many times that happened. We spent three hours on the Atlantic City beach one morning with Alan watching every move made by a guy near us. Alan would tell me to look every time the guy would roll over, stand up, or sit down. He was over 6 ft. tall, but so am I. and that doesn't really impress me. It was obvious that he lifted weights and had a muscular body that impressed Alan. A muscular body is attractive to me until they take it too far and start looking like apes. He looked like an ape. It only took Alan a few minutes to approach him after the beach crowd made its regular transfer to the Chester Inn. I sat at the bar near a fellow that I thought was nice and Alan showed up with his beach choice. Things were getting more exciting for Alan as the conversation brought out his friends address in the vicinity of our home. Immediately after Alan went to the men's room, his heart throb asked me if there were ever times that I was home without Alan. The guy that had my interest, heard the conversation and wanted to rearrange our seating so that Alan would be next to him and I would be next to Alan's heart throb. Sometimes it worked out right, but this was one of the usual ones that worked out backwards.

Chapter 15 - The Years in Our First House

Dad called me and suggested that I look at some houses that were for sale because he was always interested in investments. They were newly constructed homes on large lots in a country neighborhood. Alan and I were both making good money and I bought one. I paid for the house, but it was easy to do with Alan paying half of our expenses. The house was just outside of a little town in a remote area near McGuire Air Force Base. McGuire Air Force Base was adjacent to Fort Dix, mom and dad's meeting place. I was about to live a mile from the town that started it all. There were actually 3 small towns on the perimeter of the 2 military bases.

Mom mentioned a bar called the Pig and Whistle in one of the towns called Brown's Mills. I had to take an afternoon ride through Browns Mills and look for this bar. It was on the outside of town on a back road through the New Jersey Pine barrens and sat all by itself in a desolate area. It was early afternoon and there were very few customers, so I went inside and ordered a beer. As I looked around the room, I tried to imagine my mother and father as young customers during the 1940's. Mom played the perfect mother during my childhood and would not even eat dinner in a restaurant that was half bar. This was entirely bar and hardly the type of place that I could picture my mother visiting. It was by her own admission and I was sure that she had been there. It made me see another side of my mother that I did not really look down on. To the contrary, I somewhat envied her because I would love to be an attraction in a room full of young soldiers and I tried to imagine what it was like during her youth.

There were several back roads that went further into the unpopulated remote areas all around our home. Alan and I bought bicycles and started taking rides on the back roads. Alan said that we should take our clothes off and get a complete tan, so that was how we rode bikes. There was something sexy about being outside naked and we even stopped to play on a few occasions.

Dad and Mom showed up at the house and said that they came over for a swim in our pool. Alan did not know them because I had been staying away from them and this was our first meeting in more than a year. Mom brought a pot roast and said that she had dinner for us. It seemed like it was going to be a rough evening when Alan told me to get my mother out of his kitchen, but things calmed down and we wound up playing cards. Then we received a Friday night invitation to dinner and cards at their house and I couldn't believe that Alan wanted to go. It became a regular routine for us to play cards at alternating homes. Mom did not really swear, but she would occasionally slip and say "shit". Dad didn't like it and she tried not to slip, but it came out in our card game. We played a game called "Oh Hell" that required bidding the number of tricks that you would take. Every time my mother got stuck with a trick that she didn't expect, she would slip with the word "shit". It made Alan and I laugh so much that dad finally started laughing too. I think we were making her take tricks so that we could hear her say "shit".

After 25 years of living in the same town with my mother's oldest brother and never speaking to him, dad saw him and invited him to a Friday night card game. The family problem never involved him and we didn't do anything wrong, but his wife would not let him speak to us. Her youngest son wasn't related to my uncle and she was the only problem. He came to the card game and we had a great night. Mom was very happy that it happened because he died a short time later and she did get to see him before he died. It was very strange for dad to have invited him after so many years of silence and it happened just in time. The son that wasn't his, had more love for him than for his mother, which had to say something good about my uncle.

One weekday afternoon Mom and Dad showed up at my house when I got home from work. Dad started with, "We just got some bad news". The doctor had just told them that mom had colon cancer. She went into my office and used the phone to call a friend that was also diagnosed with colon cancer. They spoke on the phone for nearly an hour and mom was somewhat convinced that it could be removed.

A few weeks later, she went into the Trenton hospital, were I was born, because a doctor friend of theirs worked in that hospital. I wasn't too impressed with the hospital and thought that the University of Penn in Philadelphia would be much safer. I went to the hospital after the operation and she told me that the colon tumor had attached to her bladder and they didn't have a doctor that could do the bladder operation, so they closed her back up. She knew that cutting into cancer and not removing it would mean the end. Sometimes ignorance is bliss and it hurts to know too much. She knew and she was right. Dad had gone home during the operation to take a shower. The hospital also said that they could not find my father for permission to do the second operation. Mom got really mad at dad and asked him how he could possibly have gone home. I am sure that it must have made dad feel terrible, but nothing made any sense except my assumption that the University of Penn was a better hospital. Why would you need permission to do an operation if you didn't have a doctor available? They had permission to do an operation for the removal of cancer. Did they need a separate signature for each place they cut after they open you up? There should have been a malpractice lawsuit because even my mother knew that it would be better to have some bed pan nurse remove the bladder with a butter knife than to close and guarantee termination. The only accurate thing that they did was to predict five more years which came true.

Mom and Dad both retired and started spending half of the year in a Florida home. We visited them in Florida at Christmas and didn't tell them that we were in Florida for spring break at the gay Marlin Beach Hotel every Easter. Before I met Alan, I went to Florida for spring breaks and as we approached our first Easter together, it was the first time that I was suggesting a trip. Alan usually came up with the things that we did, but this one was mine. and he wasn't hard to convince. We continued the annual trek for the next ten years. The Marlin had a bar manager that Alan could not resist. I agreed that he was pretty hot. Rory was a tall, well built, long haired blond with a nice tan. If we were on the balcony and Rory was crossing the courtyard, we had to stop and watch. One year, we sat down on the airplane for our return trip to New Jersey and we saw Wayne come through the door. Alan said that he hoped Wayne would not see us. Well he did, and as Alan feared, he screamed Hi girls' with his arms waving in the air. Alan said that he was going to try and climb under the seat where nobody could see him.

The Marlin Beach hotel was a great attraction that I really miss. It was directly on the beach with a dining room view of the ocean. It caused two blocks of the beach to be entirely gay and when you walked out on the beach somebody would usually call, hi girl, come on over here. The four story, square building, surrounded an open courtyard in the center with a pool and patio bar. The main bar was a big square with one side facing through the dining room and out to the ocean while the other side was windows to the pool. You could sit at the bar and see boys in bathing suits on the beach and turn to see more at the pool. There was another bar in the basement that had large, underwater windows to the pool. One night, a couple checked into the hotel at a late hour. They noticed that nobody was on the dimly lit pool patio and decided to skinny dip. They had no idea that there were underwater windows with 200 people watching. Alan and I heard them say that they were going to skinny dip and we had to go down and see the bar reaction. The pool had a diving board at the end near the windows. One of the guys was hanging from the diving board with his naked body swinging against the underwater window. There was so much screaming that the security guard at the door upstairs could hear the commotion and proceeded to investigate. He told the guests about the windows and we never saw them again. The guard should have told them that the bar customers liked what they saw and maybe they would have stayed.

An Easter parade went past the front of the Marlin Beach Hotel during one of our visits. Hundreds of gay guys were sitting on the front porch of the Marlin Beach Hotel with even more at Ocean front windows in the rooms above. The opposite side of the street was filled with gay guys from the beach who were watching the straight people's parade. A local gym had entered a float in the parade that had six of their guys in bathing suits. The hundreds of gay guys screamed and whistled at the men on the float. One of the guys from the float jumped down and held up a girl from the spectator crowd. He said, "try this ". There was a spontaneous Boo from hundreds of guys that must have been heard in Miami. It sure was the opposite extreme from my old days in the closet of the 1950's and I was loving it.

The government had made significant changes in payroll taxes one year and I had to work through the Christmas holiday and change computer programs in 18 school districts. I called my mother in Florida and said that I would have to work through the holiday and could not come down for Christmas. She said, "Can't Alan come either" I couldn't wait to tell him that he got invited to Florida without me. Alan and I had a very understanding relationship and never really had a serious fight about anything. We were considerate to each other and I would have

let him go to Florida alone, if he really wanted to.
Alan was good for me because I am somewhat
conservative and he got me to do things that I
would not have done without him. He wanted to
see Grace Jones perform at Fire Island and
talked me into driving my Cadillac out Long
Island. Everyone seemed to know everyone else
on Fire Island and I felt very left out because I
was not a part of this family of friends. We
didn't realize it, but the last boat returns at
midnight and there are no hotels on Fire Island.
In fact, there are no streets, no cars, no stores
and nothing but a few bars, luncheonette and
boardwalks through the woods to beautiful
homes on the sand dunes. Fortunately, the
weather was great and we just slept on the
beach.

I later got to know many of the people that
owned those beautiful homes and would receive
invitations to return. Unfortunately, Alan was
no longer with me when I met the residents and
without his push, I never made it back to Fire
Island. I have watched the movie about Fire
Island more than five times and always feel like I
have missed something. I never would have
made the original trip alone, but really enjoyed
what is a very unique place.

Alan wanted to see a play in York City, so we
took the train to New York. We were standing
in the Ticketron line without any particular
show in mind and someone offered to sell us
tickets to Ol Calcutta. The Ticketron line was
long, so we bought the tickets. They turned out

to be front row seats in a play that had great looking nude males. We made many trips to New York and even took the Hudson River cruise. West Point was a must see for two gay boys.

Every time that we did not feel like cooking, we took the back country roads to an old farm house that had been converted to a restaurant overlooking a country lake. The owner's son was another Bud and a very friendly, good looking bartender. Bud was one of our attractions to the restaurant. We would sit at the bar and drink while dinner was being prepared. It was a beautiful, antique, carved wood bar in a fantastic room lit by tiffany lamps and even had a Nickelodeon that worked for a nickel. We would be called to our own table by a window overlooking the lake when our dinner was on our regular table. It was particularly great on winter nights when people were skating on the lake and sledding on the hill behind the lake directly outside of our table by the window. One room of the restaurant was set up as a salad bar with a variety of homemade breads. The food was great and we both loved going there. On one occasion, I felt bad because we were in the middle of a wedding reception eating king crab and lobster while the wedding reception was served the usual wedding special chicken.

Alan was an extremely handsome, young person that always wanted to be an actor. He was 10 years younger than me and looked 10 years younger than he actually was. His thick black hair always looked combed and he was always combing it anyway. I met him while he was in his second year at the county college and was invited to see him in many plays at the college. He made good money working with computers, but constantly took singing lessons, dancing lessons and anything that might be useful in acting. I never discouraged him because I didn't want it to be my fault if he never reached his goal in life and I even tried to teach him how to sing. The ultimate sacrifice was when I helped him move to New York City to study at the Barbizon School of modeling. He rented a room from a gay guy in New York City. I drove him to his new room and met the roommate who owned the apartment. He did not make a good first impression and I was worried about what Alan was getting himself into. One night at 11:00, I was awakened from bed by a telephone call from Alan. He had locked himself in his room and was scared of the landlord who wanted more than a tenant. You had to see the nasty old bird in order to appreciate why Alan was scared. I made the hour car trip to New York City in half an hour. The Nellie old queen let me into the third floor apartment and started to argue with me. Alan came out of his room and I told him to put his things in the car that I left in the middle of the street. He stepped between Alan and the outside door. I told him to stand over by the windows and shut his mouth until we left because I was getting real close to throwing him through the fucking window. It wasn't difficult to see that I was angry enough to throw him out the window and he took the quiet position while we left. The only regret that I have is that I could not help him find the break that he needed to reach his dream, but I am happy to say that I never did anything to discourage it. I can say that he was a handsome guy that everybody found attractive and sometimes that is a majority of what you need for an actor's part.

We discovered the very gay town of New Hope, Pennsylvania and started spending a lot of time there. It was a beautiful old town on the Delaware River with the usual gay setting of antique shops. There was an old canal through town that had once been used by donkey drawn barges. The canal was not in use anymore, but the gays used the underside of bridges over the canal at night. Our favorite place was a farm that had been converted to a gay club called the Cartwheel. The original barn had several bars, a large dance floor and disco music. There was an underground tunnel to the cellar of the farm house where they had a leather bar. The first floor of the farm house had several bars including a piano bar where customers sang show tunes. You know where Alan could always be found. I would wander around the club and eventually join Alan at the piano. There was another bar on the same road called the Prelude, but we seldom selected that one. After the clubs closed at 2:00 am, everybody went to a diner at the edge of town. The diner was straight all day, but the gays took over after the bars closed. A leftover straight couple were finishing their food when the gay crowd arrived one night. Six guys sat at a table next to the straight couple. One of the guys said that he was going to the ladies room and another guy responded that they wouldn't be seeing him for awhile if he finds the glory hole. The straight couple finished eating faster than obese people eat. The girl didn't have anything to worry about except losing her boyfriend, but the guy had something to worry about.

Alan insisted that we take my mother and father out to dinner on her birthday. He picked a five star restaurant in New Hope called Chez Odette. I knew that this was not going to meet with my father's approval because he always read a menu from right to left. If the price was okay, he would read the entree on that line. He wasn't going to be reading any entrees on the Chez Odette menu. The bill for cocktails was $70 and that would be twice what Dad normally paid for an entire dinner. I was uncomfortable because when the waiter came, it was love at first sight. Wouldn't you know that when I was out with my family and lover, this waiter gave me a suggestive smile that almost made me jump on him in front of everyone. Dad complained that it was too dark in there and he couldn't see how much salt he was putting on his food. I knew that the complaints would continue throughout the night. The final complaint came while the valet was getting our car and it was his real complaint. He said that he could buy a kitchen for what it cost to eat in that restaurant.

Alan and I returned to the Chez Odette

restaurant a few months later in a terrible rainstorm. It was difficult to see in the poorly lighted parking lot with the heavy rain and I took the wrong lane when leaving. We almost drove into a deep canal when I realized that the highway shouldn't be that far away and we were on the wrong road. Then we saw a news report saying that our weather girl and her date were drowned when they made a wrong turn and drove into a canal at a New Hope restaurant. I hate to think that I could have prevented a drowning if we had reported our problem with the driveways, but I fear that it is the case. There are things that you would prefer to forget and will always remember. This will be one for me.

Mom and Dad decided to reciprocate and take us out to dinner on Alan's birthday. We went to their favorite diner called the Golden Moon. Alan was giving the waitress his order and requested the house dressing on his salad. I burst into laughter and said, "House Dressing! Dad is taking us out to dinner and we are in a diner, you can get vinegar and oil or French". It wasn't a very nice thing for me to do, but after I thought about it, I was glad that I made a point of what you don't get when you don't pay the prices that were on our Chez Odette menu. I did restrain myself to stop from saying that after you eat at Chez Odette you could have bought a kitchen and before you eat at the Golden Moon, you should have bought a kitchen. Alan and I were not above going to diners and the food actually was good. We went to a diner in our own neighborhood and an obese couple was coming out as we entered. I told Alan that it was a waste of our time to go in because they would be out of food after serving those two. Alan ordered something and the waitress said that she was sorry, but they were out of that. It was the first time that the waitress ever saw customers laugh right off the seat over the diner being out of something. Her line was better than a good comedy show after what I had said in the entrance. This was a diner where we enjoyed the entertainment more than the dinner and they didn't even have entertainment.

Alan's next venture, after trying to get into acting, was to apply for a position with the Chess King clothing chain. He commuted to New York City by train for a while and worked as a purchasing agent. It was great for me because they had auctions to sell the samples that they received from manufacturers. Alan got leather coats for me at $5 each and they would retail for $300 each. I had leather in every color and style imaginable along with a complete Chess King wardrobe. Alan told me that all of my clothes looked like horse blankets. He was right. I liked the dull earthen colors and even if I picked a plaid, it would be multiple shades of brown. He was picking my clothes for me and I actually liked the variety that I never would have selected. I would pick him up at the Princeton junction train station and always ask if I should bring the car or the truck. The company asked him to work as an assistant manager for six months and then they would give him his own store. His assistant position was in Delaware and as usual, I agreed to help him with this step in a new career. He rented an apartment in Delaware and I suggested that he take any furniture that he wanted from the house because we were planning on purchasing new furniture anyway. We made a few truck trips to Delaware and he got most of the living room and dining room furniture.

Chapter 16 - Living Alone Again

We had talked about buying new furniture and had decided on what we wanted. I was without furniture and had to go out and buy it. Every other weekend, Alan would come home and on the opposite weekends, I would visit him in Delaware. The first weekend that he returned home, he was upset because I had furnished the entire house with exactly what he wanted, after he was gone. I told him that this is exactly what we said we were going to do and that he would only be in Delaware for six months.

I also had a brown Cadillac that Alan never liked. The day that I brought it home, he asked me why I bought that color. It was 3 years old and I wanted to trade it because it was out of warranty. I traded the cheap, Brown Coupe de Ville for an expensive, white, Eldorado Barritz with a special red, cut leather interior and stainless steel roof. I just liked the car and bought it because that is what I did every three years. The following weekend was my turn to go to Delaware and I realized that Alan might get upset over this car like he did with the furniture. I didn't park anywhere near his apartment when I got there. We were inside for a few hours and Alan said that we should go somewhere for lunch. This did not seem like it would be a problem because I could ask Alan to drive in a city that he knew and was strange to me. He agreed and we went out toward his car. Typically observing Alan said that he didn't see my car, where did I park? I told him that the car was at the end of the row and as I might have expected, he checked the end of the row. I finally had to tell him that it wasn't the old brown car because my three years were up and I had to trade.

Back at home, a young couple rented the house next to mine and were moving in. They were from Texas, which qualified them to be my friends. Danny could be described as a stocky guy with a boyish face and a full head of beautiful brown hair. He wasn't overweight, just built like a bull. The thin blond girlfriend was not his wife and her two preschool children were from a former relationship. Guys must have selected old, worn and shrunken jeans for cutting off legs to make shorts because they always seemed to be too small. Danny's shorts were too small for his body even though they were the right size for catching my attention. Our yards were oversized country lots and it took him all day to cut the lawn with his 18 inch lawnmower. My lawn tractor did the job in half an hour. Danny and I both started to cut our lawns one Saturday morning. I finished mine and he still had most of his to cut. I waved him over to my fence and said that I would swing over and do his lawn if he would open my double gate. You never saw a gate opened so fast. He went into the house and came back out with a beer for me. It was the perfect way for me to meet him because he wanted to make sure that we became friendly enough for me to cut his lawn the next time I did mine. His girlfriend was nice and he liked her cute kids, but he started coming over to my house to watch football games because he couldn't do it at home. I played almost every sport, but hated to watch somebody else doing it and I normally wouldn't watch a football game. To me, it was like going to a restaurant to watch the other people eat. Alan was in Delaware and I didn't have anything else to do except sit there with Danny, so I watched football games. Actually, Danny was aware of all of the moves being made by players on my television screen, but I was more aware of the moves being made by the guest rearranging himself on my couch.

I told Danny a true story about our fat neighbors across the street. They were so fat that he would get into their big Cadillac and the driver's side would tilt down. Then she would get into the passenger side and the entire car would be down. Cadillacs have pneumatic shocks that pump the car up when there is a heavy load. When he started the motor, you could see the car coming back up again. I should have taken movies of it because it was funny. I mention them to Danny because I had offered to cut their lawn before

Danny moved in. The husband refused my offer because he needed the exercise to lose weight. I watched him push the mower with his right hand while he was eating a submarine sandwich with his left hand. After a few passes, the sandwich would be gone and he would go into the house for a piece of chocolate cake. Then he would push the mower with his right hand and eat chocolate cake with his left hand. A few more passes with the lawn mower and then it was time to stop and light the grill. They came out of their house while Danny and I were watching television and headed toward the car. In the next few minutes, they helped me to convince Danny that there are much more interesting things to watch than football. Danny moved to New Jersey because his parents did not approve of his girlfriend that already had two kids without a husband. I wanted to suggest that Danny ask his parents if they would approve of a boyfriend that could never have that problem of kids by anyone. Financial problems resulted in arguments between Danny and his girlfriend and he moved back to Texas without the girlfriend. I guess that she moved on to her next man somewhere. I missed Danny, but could finally get out the remote control and set it to delete the football station.

Alan was still in Delaware and I was going home to an empty house, so I frequently stopped at a local Inn a few blocks from home. There was a local pig farmer in there every afternoon and he always made me laugh. He liked me because I was the only person that wore a suit and tie, drove a Cadillac and talked to him. They called him big Al and that was an understatement. He had a tiny little wife and four kids. His wife was always mad at him because he finished each day by getting drunk at the bar. His stories about the trip home were always good. He was urinating on the radiator in his hallway one night and she heard him from bed. She asked him where he was and he answered that he was in the bathroom. She screamed, "no you are not". He said that he was so drunk that he didn't realize where he was and he took a wizzy in the radiator. A few nights later, he told me that he got home and climbed into bed without any problems. She didn't wake up. Then he relieved some gas, but it was more than gas that came out. That woke her up and she was really mad. It wasn't hard to imagine that she might have been a least displeased. I could do anything that I wanted in the bar because Big Al liked me and would come to my assistance. He just looked at people and said "you got a problem with that?" His idea of fun was to take on six in a good fight. The bar was full of military people and Johnny Carson was on television. Carson said that Military Intelligence is a term like Jumbo Shrimp. It was okay for me to be the only one laughing because Big Al was right next to me.

The bar air conditioning was not working one afternoon and it was hot when I arrived. There was a soldier at the bar, so I ordered a beer and sat down. I told Denise, the barmaid, that I would be having my next one in the pool at home after sitting in that heat. The soldier said that he wished he was sitting in a pool. Denise offered the information that my pool was only 3 blocks away and he said that he didn't have a bathing suit. I told him that he didn't need a suit because you couldn't see through the fences and he was welcome to take a swim. I spent the next two hours with a naked soldier and then drove him back to the base through a side gate near my home. After several more times of entertaining soldiers and returning them to the base, I took one home and the gate guard recognized my car. He stepped out of his booth and waved me through. The soldier was shocked. He said, I'm stationed here and they ID me, but you drive right through. Oh Well.

Two soldiers came into the bar on motor cycles during a rain storm. They were soaked to the skin and it stopped raining. They said that they should have waited because it wasn't raining now and they would have to ride home wet because they came in the rain. I offered to let them put their clothes in my clothes dryer and they accepted the offer. I didn't even offer them a towel while they waited for their clothes to dry in my laundry room. My mother must have been thinking about the military base when she was carrying me because I sure loved it.

My mother, father, sister and brother-in-law came to my house to see the Memorial Day air show at McGuire. They almost changed their mind because of the lines of cars that they saw going into the main gate. We slipped through the side gate and my friends brought us beer and coke while we watched the air show. I was living with a guy and displayed a familiarity with the military base, but my family still did not acknowledge the obvious fact that I was gay. Dad had a real reason to reject me now and he seemed to be accepting me. We had conversations like friends and made voluntary visits to see each other.

The six months went by very fast and Alan was back home in the new furniture and going to the beach with me in the new Cadillac. I gave him a scare with my new car. There was a button that opened the garage door from inside the house. I usually pushed it as I went out to the garage. I didn't push it one morning because a windy rainstorm was driving water across the front porch and against our living room windows. The open garage door would have let the rain blow on me and I decided to open the door from within the car. Familiar habits took over and I started the car without thinking about the closed garage door. I put the car into reverse gear and it started to move backwards as I was turning around to watch where I was going. I backed right through the closed garage door. I sat there laughing like an idiot because of what I had done and laughed even harder as Alan ran out with a look of shock on his face. There wasn't a mark on the car, but the bottom half of the wooden garage door was gone.

Alan was one of the best things that ever happened to me and having known him gives me a great deal of comfort because our relationship excludes me from being one of the many people who lived their entire life alone. You might say that he saved me from being the gay equivalent to an old maid. Like most gay men, we spent a lot of time creating a beautiful home. We were opposites and that was an advantage. Alan created beautiful flower gardens while I was the one that rode the lawn tractor. He had to do all of the painting because my finished paint job was worse than before I started, but if his car broke down, he would leave it for me to fix. I hired a local contractor to build a custom fireplace in the house. You would normally be anxious for something like that to get finished, but it was summer and we couldn't use the fireplace and the contractor had a typical construction worker's build. It was great to watch him take his shirt off and work in cut off jeans that would have fit somebody smaller than him. The next project was a large, heated, swimming pool. The law required a 4 ft. fence around the pool. Our lot was large and I thought that it would be okay to have a fence company put a chain link fence on the perimeter of the property. The large property didn't serve the purpose that I wanted. You could see the fence and I told Alan that it made the yard look like a dog kennel. Alan fixed that by planting honeysuckle and grape vines in the fence. It not only hid the fence, but we had concord grapes. Alan followed the entertainment publications and scheduled all of our outings, but I was always the one that drove the car. If it were not for him, I would have spent a great deal more time at home, but I always enjoyed myself when he dragged me out. After 10 years of a great relationship, we moved to Florida. I had completed 20 years at the high-school and decided to vest my pension and move to Florida. I hated the winter weather and my entire family was enjoying Florida. Mom was having problems with her cancer. The radiation burned her skin and the chemotherapy made her stop eating, while the cancer kept getting worse anyway. Dad was on an unbelievable routine of staying with her 24 hours a day and giving her medication every three hours day and night. Sometimes the morphine would make her lose control of her bowels in bed and he would clean the mess. She didn't have much time left and I want it to see her and help if I could.

Chapter 17 - The Move to Florida

I went to Florida first and got established. I met a doctor who had several businesses and a computer that he did not know how to use. He offered me a small salary and "a piece of the action" to set up the computer system under a new company to manage the existing companies. He continued to open new businesses until there were 20 HMO clinics, a construction company, a mail order pharmacy, and a home nursing service. My salary grew to an acceptable income and I had a beautiful office overlooking the ocean, but a piece of the action was never clearly defined. We rented a majority of the offices on the first two floors of a 20 story condominium building.

Alan followed and went to work for me and the
doctor. It was great at first. We had an
oceanfront condominium with a spectacular view
and felt like we were on vacation all the time.
Our ocean front condominium building was
right on the boardwalk in Hollywood, Florida.
The first floor was rented to a bar, a restaurant,
and a delicatessen. There was always a young
crowd on our beach because of the bar and deli.
Hollywood allows drinking on the beach and the
bar would serve beach drinks in plastic. Young
guys liked the area because they could buy a six
pack in the deli and drink cheap. We could see a
pay phone on the boardwalk from our 14th floor
balcony. When somebody was near the phone, I
would call it from the balcony and have some
fun. There was a girl near the phone in a pizza
restaurant uniform. I called and she answered
the phone. I asked for a pizza delivery and she
was really confused. She was looking all around
but never looked straight up 14 floors. She had
her eye on a guy in a red bathing suit. She told
me that she couldn't take an order because she
was not at work. I told her to forget about the
boys in red bathing suits on the beach and get to
work. This really had her looking around.

Alan and I rode bikes on the boardwalk and
went to our beach bar every day. It strained our
relationship to be together 24 hours a day, but I
think we could have survived that problem.
Alan did not get along with my doctor partner
and that compounded the problem. The doctor

was really a great guy if you got to know him, but Alan never did.   Doc asked Alan to run a financial statement for one of the clinics at 4:30. Alan ran the statement without saying a word to doc and waited until we were home to tell me that my fucking partner asked him to run a financial statement that takes an hour and it was closing time.   The next day, I told the doctor not to ask Alan for another hour's work at closing time.   Doc said that he didn't realize it was closing time and I am sure it was true because he never lived by the clock. His schedule was a crazy mad house of activities and it was my job to organize the results. One of our doctors called me and asked why I did not include a paycheck for the cleaning lady at his clinic. I didn't even know that there was a cleaning lady and asked Doc if he had hired someone.   He said, " oh yeah, I forgot to tell you about her ". He opened his wallet and pulled out a matchbook cover with all of the information.   This was just doc and his wild world of business activities.   I told him that I needed to talk to him one day and he said that he had to leave because he was taking his wife to the airport and he was late. He told me to come with him and talk in the car. We arrived at the airport a few minutes before flight time. He and his wife jumped out of the car and he told me to drive around the airport a few times while he put his wife on the plane. His car phone rang and I answered it. It was our bookkeeper Doug calling from the office. Doug recognized my voice and was totally confused because he had called the car phone. I told him that I was in doc's car at the airport and he said that he just saw me in the office a few minutes ago. I said that I was in the office a few minutes ago, but you know what it is like working with Doc and I am in the airport now. We both started to laugh and I never did find out what Doug wanted.

Alan and I had no financial problems and I suggested that he quit and return to school or find a different job, but he continued to work for me. At the same time, we were entertaining ourselves at a square dance bar. I didn't square dance, so he danced with another guy that had more of an interest than dancing. One evening, just before Christmas, the dancing partner convinced Alan that they should leave the area together. They disappeared from the bar and drove to California together. I thought that Alan must have walked home, so I went home to find him. He wasn't there and I spent the next few hours driving around the area to find him. Our longtime relationship of trust had ended and I was feeling mixed emotions of sadness and anger. It was hard to believe that he left without telling me that he was going. It was partially my fault, because I told his dance partner that I should break every bone in his body for making a pass at somebody that was not available. Their relationship lasted a very short time and Alan returned to another area in Florida. I got his telephone number from his father and called him. He was not very receptive on the telephone and I never called again. The incident has made Christmas and upsetting time of the year. I can still feel the pain of wondering what to do with all the Christmas presents that I bought for him that year. Once again, I tend to put some of the blame on my father. The way that I was raised made me very poor at expressing my emotions and I am sure that I could have done a better job of letting Alan know how I felt about him. His dancing partner didn't have much competition in that regard.

My condo held too many bad memories and I was working in an office building that was selling condominiums. I bought a condominium on the floor above our offices and was able to take an elevator to work. It was a gigantic and beautiful Condominium with four sliding glass doors that opened to a balcony over the intercoastal waterway. The ocean was directly across the street and had a tiki hut bar on the sand. There was a grocery store and a shopping center within walking distance. Everything that I needed was right there and I seldom left the area. Alan was gone, but his mother continued to write to me from New Jersey. She had been ill while we were still living in New Jersey and she came to stay with us for a few months. We became very friendly and her letters were more personal than any conversations that I ever had with my own family. Alan called me for the first time since he left and said that his mother had died and he would be returning to New Jersey for the funeral. I would have gone too, but was not invited. She had evidently written a letter to me and mailed it just before she died. I received the letter after Alan's telephone call and it was hard to read her friendly comments and advice as though it was coming from her grave.

A new bar opened under the name "Club Shadows". I was living alone in the big condo and my bookkeeper was gay. We started going to Club Shadows after work and who do I find, but Marlin Beach manager Rory. In all the times we watched Rory, we had never met or spoken to him. He sat by me and I could not resist telling him about Alan and all the years that Alan admired him. Rory explained that he took a job as an airline steward and sometimes had a layover in Ft. Lauderdale. He made a remark to the effect that he needed to find a place where he could stay when in Lauderdale. I should have jumped on that remark with an invitation to my guest room, but it was always hard for me to say something that might seem like a pass. It was just that old inferiority complex that makes it safer to shut up than open a door to rejection. It was great to have finally met this idol that we admired for so many years and his personality was so casual that I actually felt like one of his good friends at the end of our afternoon together.

James, my computer supplier from New Jersey, came down for a visit and stayed with me in the condo. I showed him the offices and he met my bookkeeper, Doug. Doug was infatuated with James, but I explained that he was straight and would be staying in the guest room. James and I went to the beach bars and woke up still drunk in my bed. I had to correct my information to Doug because James didn't sleep in the guest room. Some months later, James returned to

Florida with his wife. They visited James's mother, who spent winters in Florida, but stayed in my condo with me. I told Doug that James was here, but I would be sleeping alone this time because he brought his wife Lois. James, Lois and I watched television until a late hour and Lois said that she was going to bed. She left us and went into the guest room. Sometime later, I told James that I was tired and going to bed too. He said that he would come with me because he didn't want to wake Lois up. I couldn't wait to tell Doug who slept alone that night. We enjoyed a week at the beach and straight beachfront bars, but it was nice to be back into the gay crowd after they left.

Closing each day with a trip to Club Shadows was much better than going home to an empty condo at 5:00 pm. It wasn't so bad in New Jersey winters with darkness approaching at 5, but 5 pm in summertime Florida is still a bright part of the day and just doesn't encourage going home and ending your day's activity. I am sure that it would be different if I had a family at home and going home would be the beginning of family activity, but that is not an option for gay people. Many protestant ministers would use this as a reason to like women and change to a straight life. They seem to think that it is a choice like selecting an entry from a dinner menu. It would actually ruin the lives of two partners that could never share the physical attraction and sexual interests of a heterosexual relationship. The bar offered some social activity that I needed. Drinking was never a factor and I usually ordered something mild that I would nurse for a long time. When somebody would insist on buying me a shot of whisky, I would say that I came out to be out and not to pass out. There is something different about alcoholics and I doubt very much if that is a learned trait because I drank daily and never felt a need for liquor. In fact, there was always liquor at home and I never wanted to drink it in the absence of entertaining company. I've had friends that would wake up in the middle of the night for a drink. One of my friends could start drinking a Vodka and water at 10:00 am. There is no way that I could put anything stronger than black coffee and toast in my mouth at 10:00 am. I have other friends that do not crave a drink, but after they have a few drinks, it is impossible for them to stop. When I start getting sloppy or sleepy from alcohol, I need to get back to my bed and I have no difficulty stopping. One of my friends does not drive and would join me anytime that I would provide the transportation. Although I enjoy his company, I never provide his transportation because he always wants to have just one more and when I need to go home I do not want just one more drop. I have even stopped and let him have more while I sat there in discomfort and waited. His need is so uncontrolled, that he would let me sit while he continued drinking until he fell on the floor.

Alan and I originally met my bookkeeper, Doug, in the infamous square dance bar of our demise. He was a part time bartender and looking for a job. His background was telephone company employee and he knew nothing about business offices. I hired him and taught him bookkeeping. He and his gay lover became two of my best and most trusted friends in Florida. We went to a company Christmas Party together and Doug got pulled away to dance with an ugly, fat, old nurse who worked with us. I told his lover Ken, that it was a good thing Doug was gay because his taste in women was pretty damned poor. We spent the entire night laughing over similar remarks. Doug learned everything very fast and easily found another job when we both left the company.

The doctor said that we were moving the business and he needed all the employees to stay after work on Friday evening. Our lease agreement was an escalating contract for two years at below market rate, the third year at market rate, and the last two years would be above market value to compensate for the first two years. I told the doctor that we still had two years left on the lease and he asked me what corporation signed the lease. I reminded him that the lease was under FTW Corp. Then he asked me if I knew what FTW stood for. He spent $30 to register the corporation name FTW which had no assets and stood for fuck the world. The trucks pulled up and under the cover of darkness everything was removed, right down to the last pencil sharpener on the wall. He was a good teacher because this is the way business is done in Florida and something I had never learned in New Jersey.

The new offices were in Hialeah. It was a long drive for me and not a very pleasant place to work. It was actually a big warehouse that was partitioned into offices. There was still some irritation about "peace of the action " and subsequent to a heated telephone conversation, I was only with the company a short time longer. Mom was becoming increasingly ill and difficult for dad. She was totally bedridden and could not cook for them any longer. Dad had never even made a sandwich for himself. I was living in the condo where my business partner had created serious problems by walking out on the lease. Consequently, I sold the condo, moved in with Dad and Mom, and went into real estate sales. The next year was very rough for me and I realized what Dad was going through. Mom needed to eat and the chemotherapy destroyed her appetite. She would tell me that she might be able to eat some spaghetti and I would cook spaghetti. When it was done, she would apologize and say that she couldn't eat it after smelling it cooking. It would upset her and she would start crying. I started cooking everything on the grill outside so that she would not be able to smell it before it was served. It reached a point where the morphine was not stopping the pain and she had to go into the hospital. Her youngest brother came down to visit her because we knew it was very near the end. She held a finger to her chest and told him to please shoot me right here. Many years ago, when we were all living in New Jersey, she had a small dog that was suffering from arthritis. Pain made the dog cry every time he moved. Mom called me and asked me to take the dog to the veterinarian to be put to sleep. She could not do it herself, but could not allow him to continue living in pain. That memory came back to me as I saw her lying in worse pain then she would allow for her dog. Dad, Uncle Tom, and my sister left the hospital to get something for dinner just before I arrived. Mom died while I was there and I have always been grateful that I was there and she did not die alone. It seems terrible to say this, but it was the easiest way to lose someone because it would be the only way that you could be glad to see someone die. Mom had always been a very independent person who had done everything for everyone else. If I had a 5:00 a.m. appointment and my sister left the house at 6 and Dad got up at 7, Mom would fix breakfast three times without a word of complaint. She spent the past two years in a total loss of dignity as she couldn't even take care of her own toilet needs.

I had just gained some respect for my father because of his loyalty to my mother in the terrible time that he went through for her. He was good to my mother, but he was about to put me back in my place. I moved to a beach front apartment and his parting words were, "this is the last time that you move out and if you get sick, don't come back here". Six months later, he got married again.

Chapter 18 - The Stepmother

My mother and father had some of the characteristics of Archie and Edith Bunker. She wouldn't know how to reset a circuit breaker if the power went off and he didn't know how to make a peanut butter and jelly sandwich. My sister Susan and I visited him shortly after my mother died. He was sitting on his living-room couch totally exhausted and explained that he had just finished vacuuming the carpets. We looked at the carpets and started to laugh because there were lines where he had vacuumed in rows as you would cut a lawn. Susan tried to explain how he should stand in one spot and vacuum around himself.

I could understand how he would have difficulty trying to live alone, but it was impossible for me to imagine him getting married again. I never really knew him and he was about to prove it. About six months after my mother died, Dad showed up at my sister's house and announced that he got married again. Susan was slightly relieved to think that she would not have to continue fixing all his meals, but she did not approve. The idea of him getting married without telling her in advance seemed somewhat suspicious to her. They had always been very close to each other and she had no reservations about telling him what she thought. She asked him why he bothered getting married at his age, did he plan on having more children? Dad tried to make her feel more comfortable about the marriage by telling her that they signed a prenuptial agreement.

Susan called me with the information and let me know that she was furious about it. The secret wedding didn't seem right to me, but I was more open minded about it then my sister was being. I told Susan that it was his decision and he didn't want to live alone. She proceeded to tell me that the new wife was considerably younger than dad and must be a gold digger because Dad wasn't the easiest person to get along with. I couldn't argue with that statement, but I was willing to give her the benefit of doubt. My sister and I were always very candid with each other and I told her that it was his money and his business if he wanted to buy a piece of ass with it. Susan corrected me on that statement. Mom always worked and paid most of the family expenses so that Dad could invest most of his money. The money that he had was because of Mom and she would not approve of him making a fool of himself. Susan was making me suspicious too, but I wasn't convinced that she was absolutely right.

Mom and Dad had always been very close to my sister's son who was just entering his teens. Dad had always promised to take the grandson Brad to New York City and visit the Statue of Liberty. Dad and his new wife were planning a trip to New York to visit family members that she had in that area. Brad wanted to go because they promised him a trip to New York, but Dad said that they didn't want to take children with them. Susan said that she would put Brad on an airplane and they could meet him in New York for a trip to the Statue of Liberty. They did meet Brad in New York City and they took him to the Statue of Liberty, but the wife's niece was with them because they allowed this younger girl on the trip that was not suppose to include children. It is a good thing that they were in New York, because Susan was mad enough to slap both of them right in the face. I had to take my sister side in the argument on this issue.

When they returned to Florida, my father tried to make my sister feel guilty about the fact that she would not accept his new wife. I have to give my sister a lot of credit for visiting them and trying to accept what my father had done. My sister's visit to their house was making it even worse because the wife had removed every picture of our family from dad's house. Brad's school pictures had been replaced by pictures of the wife's niece.

I didn't like to visit them because the new wife always wanted to hug and kiss you when you arrived. It was far too late to make this a comfortable way for our family to behave.

Susan and my brother-in-law took them out for a boat ride. They were embarrassing my sister by sitting in the open boat hugging and kissing during the entire day. This was really strange for my father who never kissed my mother in our presence during her entire lifetime.

Dad was the one who always ate in a diner and read the menu from right to left. Now he was eating in restaurants that Alan might consider to be too expensive. His vacations with Mom were car trips to places where they received free rooms for visiting a sales promotion. Now he was flying to Europe for his vacations. The only jewelry that he ever wore was a watch and now he was showing me rings that he bought for $10,000. The new wife had owned some properties and she transferred all of them to her own family members. The prenuptial agreement allows Dad to keep anything that he had when they entered the marriage and the community property is only the things that they purchase after the marriage. He had an expensive home when they entered the marriage and they sold that without ever telling me that they were going to put it on the market. Now he is talking about buying another house, which would be community property.

It would be wrong for me to stay friendly with my father so that I can get an inheritance from him, but it would be much worse for a second wife to marry him so that my mother's many years of work contributed to the inheritance of some other woman's family. My sister will surely provide the legal action to stop that from happening and I am not looking forward to the probability that I will support my sister in any argument with an outsider.

Chapter 19 - My Gay Resort

Part time involvement in real-estate sales led me to a gay hotel complex that was not listed with a realtor, but for sale. The owner was an elderly lady that bought the complex for her son. There was considerable evidence that he was so involved in narcotics that they were losing the business. She leased the club to three local gay businessmen and they changed to a gay clientele. They were doing fine and their lease was paying her bills until disputes between the three tenants caused them to walk out. She tried to run it as a gay club and didn't have any success. She hired a gay bar manager named John, but kept him on such a tight financial limitation that the business continued to fail. I could not get her to list the property because she would not pay a real estate commission, but she was having so many financial problems that I was able to purchase the property at a below market price. I called my old friend James and we purchased it together. Alan and I lived in the closet for 10 years because I worked for a school district in a very narrow minded time. He would have loved the resort because I was out of the closet and hardly ever out of the gay community. He really would have been useful to me because the complex provided entertainment to crowds that frequently exceeded a thousand people. It involved decorating and everything that Alan was good at and liked. I was even scheduled to be the grand marshal at the annual gay parade. Alan would have died to get that opportunity and I nearly died at the thought of possibly being stuck with it. I once asked Alan not to hang a nude male calendar in the house because it might be seen by the wrong person. I wonder if he knows that I owned the largest gay complex in southeast Florida and was frequently pictured in the gay magazines. There isn't a place that I can go without seeing people who know me as the kahuna of the gay community.

On my first visit to the club with its former owner and bar manager John, I wanted to sit at the bar and observe the business. The owner told me to take notice of the bartender because her son thought that he was stealing. I returned to see her in the motel office and said that I watched the bartender and didn't see any theft. The motel desk clerk reported my conversation to John and he wanted to know who the hell it was who spied on his bartender. He eventually found out who I was and had no reservations about telling me that his bartenders were none of my fucking business. This was the way that I met someone who would eventually become one of my best friends.

The gay resort complex was a very exciting time for the entire town. People constantly ask me to open another one because they miss it. I miss seeing the guests that returned from Germany, England, Canada, South America and most of all, Fire Island. Fire Island always closes for the winter and it gave us many guests that stayed for months. One of the regular Fire Island guests was an elderly man with the nickname Peaches. John knew him from his New York days and was one of the reasons that Peaches came every year to stay for several weeks. Peaches didn't drive and found our resort convenient because he never had to leave the property. We provided five bars, a motel, and a beautiful restaurant. The waterfront grounds had a swimming pool, volleyball courts, sun decks and secluded walk ways that challenged the legality of our operations at night. We had a patio bar on the pool deck and an indoor bar adjacent to the pool. Our guests insisted that we leave the large windows open and have two sides of the indoor bar opened to the pool. 40 tons of air conditioning ran constantly to keep the open room cool. The main attraction was the boys in Speedo bathing suits or no suit at all. It was the opposite of sitting in a shopping center bar with one small window overlooking a parking lot at the front. The inside was almost outside. The volley ball court was in plain view and drew as much attention as the great view of the pool crowd. There was a second floor bar with a disco sound system and dance floor. The restaurant had a beautiful marble bar under a skylight ceiling supported by wooden beams covered with tropical plants. One of the dining rooms offered the privacy of booths surrounded by brass rails that enhanced the natural brick floor. An elevated dining area was more formal with carpeting and tables. French glass doors opened to a front patio of 50 seats under a canopy with flower gardens, trees and a barbecue pit.

Peaches came to me one morning and complained that there were beer cans by the front door of his room for the past three days and nobody cleaned them up. We became very friendly and he constantly invited me to visit his beautiful home on Fire Island. One summer night, he called from Fire Island and insisted that I visit. I asked him if he was willing to throw some beer cans by the front door so that I could feel at home. He told me that it wasn't necessary for me to live in a dump all year because he learned to enjoy it as a seasonal change and I could adjust too. John told me that Peaches inherited money and never worked a day in his life. He complained constantly and I am sure that he did it because we just laughed at his complaints. John told him, "you would complain about a hair in a shit pie".

The doctor where I first worked in Florida was currently doing research on AIDS and developed a saliva testing kit for the detection of AIDS. He knew about my gay club and asked if I would find 20 volunteers that were HIV-positive who could verify the accuracy of his testing kit. I found 19 and couldn't find the 20th person. There was a shift change and I told the arriving employees that I needed someone who was HIV positive. One of the friendliest and most handsome, young desk clerks came over to me and said that he was HIV-positive. In my desperate search and without thought, I said "great". The word great was barely out of my mouth when I had realized what I said. He would be one of the last people that I would ever wish illness upon and I had just said that it was great that he was HIV-positive. I forgot everything that my family training had taught me about being unemotional and spent the next half hour trying to undo my stupid remark.

One of the bartenders that I inherited from the former owner, Scott, was a strikingly good looking Italian boy with black hair and black eyes and a handsome face. He always had a smile and was friendly with everyone while working as an excellent bartender. He was with us for a few years before he was offered a significant advancement as a food services manager. We continued to see him on occasional weekend visits to the club and it was always refreshing to greet his smiling face. I was sitting at the bar one afternoon and a customer told me that Scott had died that morning. It was impossible for me to hold back the tears as I sat there in a bar full of customers. This was the first of many times that I would see AIDS rob the world of good people in the beginning of their life and there would be many more tears coming for staff members, friends, and customers.

John and I would meet at the main bar every morning. He would check the liquor inventory while I set up the cash drawers for the day. We were about the same age, both had pilot's licenses and were both raised in the northeast. It was an exchange of stories about how flying is hours of boredom interrupted by moments of sheer panic and comparisons of our traumatic experiences in airplanes. Sometimes we would talk about New York City or Fire Island. There was always something that got us laughing. A nellie old queen that we called Coco, came in one morning and asked the bartender if anyone found a wallet the night before. He said that his date lost his wallet. John asked, " Since when are you dating people who have a wallet?" Coco was given that nickname because he was arrested twice for selling cocaine. I was told that he used as much as he sold and could never be sure if he was drunk or stoned. One day he was walking to our club from a bar a few blocks away and fell down in the street. Packets of cocaine fell from his jacket and covered the street. Fortunately for him, the ambulance attendant appreciated the gift and quickly shoved the cocaine into his own pocket before the police arrived. . The publisher of the local gay magazine was going to put our staff on his cover page. John called a staff meeting one morning, to tell the employees what sexy outfit they should wear for the cover picture. As he went around the circle, he eventually came to me and said, "And you can stay home".

The Marlin Beach Hotel closed during our second year of operation. It left us as the only full service resort in town. It meant that we should gain the Marlin customers, but I did not see it as something good for us. The Marlin was a major attraction that helped make the city a favorite place for gays. San Francisco, Toronto and Ft. Lauderdale were known as the favorite gay cities and the Marlin Beach Hotel played a big part in that evaluation. The hotel had gone through many problems in the recent years and was in poor condition at the time of closing. The gay owner died and his daughter inherited the property. Yes, gay people do have daughters and sons along with divorces and frustrated ex-wives. The daughter was an attorney and involved with politics in the northern part of the state. She did not want the problems of owning a gay hotel in a remote location and it was sold to condominium developers. It might have been sold. even if the owner had not died. It was leased to a tenant for a few years and there were many problems between the landlord and tenant. Rumors were that the tenant set the fire which destroyed the basement bar. The pool windows exploded and the flood of water extinguished the fire, but there was damage to the pool, mechanical systems in the basement and the basement bar. The owner made repairs and opened again, but the lack of routine maintenance under tenant operation was obvious to guests. The reputation that it was developing would have been as negative to the city as the closing.

John was Italian and his New York City experiences included some associations with Mafia people. Those stories were unbelievable. Don A was one of his New York City friends from years ago and was working for us as a bartender. John told me that Don's sister was John Gotti's wife. Don was late for work one day and said that his mother just came in from New York City. I asked him if she was here on a vacation and he said," no, she's here on the lamb." I didn't pursue that conversation any further. You couldn't help but enjoy Don even though he was an unattractive, elderly man. His poor health landed him in a hospital several times and the doctor always told him that he would leave the hospital feet first if he continued drinking. His first stop on the way home from the hospital was at the bar for a drink. The doctor was eventually right, but Don enjoyed himself right up to the last minute. John told me that Don had a brother and they were both such good-looking young men that people would turn to look at them when they walked down a street in New York City. It made me realize that I should be thankful for having been okay looking when I was young and not too bad as I got older because it must be devastating to have been an absolute 10 and turn into disgustingly ugly.

We had a customer that lived in a beautiful oceanfront home and came to the club in a Rolls Royce. Joe Z. never talked about the business that earned him a Rolls and I would have listened because he obviously had done something right. It was only the street people who arrived by bus that would offer suggestions on how I should be running the business. One of them was shooting pool and boasted that he was the best pool player in town. He was getting very obnoxious and annoying to the guests, so I told him that I was the worst pool player in town, but I owned the club where he had to win a pool game to get somebody to buy him a drink. That comment took the wind out of his sails and everyone else enjoyed it.

It was the first time that Joe Z. mentioned having been in the bar business. He said that he wished he had done that to a few of his customers. We continued to talk about the bar business and I mentioned the fact that my five bars were all very similar and I would like to do something that I enjoyed in a Pennsylvania bar called the Cart Wheel that had a variety of bars. Thank God that I made a complementary remark about the Cart Wheel because he proceeded to tell me that he was the former owner. I tried to picture his face in the crowd that I remembered from the Cart Wheel, but I don't think I ever met him there.

A straight guy checked into the hotel after he lost his house in a divorce settlement. He came to us because we would give him a monthly rate and he could park his boat at our motel. He also discovered that the old trolls would buy his drinks at the bar. He fell into arrears on his room rent and signed his boat title over to me as security. Things kept going down hill for him and he lost his job. His car needed repairs and his boat would not run. He wanted to sell the boat to me for $4,000 and move back to his family's home in New England. I told him that I did not want a boat and did want the $1,600 that he owed for rent. He finally told me that I could keep the boat for an additional $500 that would get him back home. The boat turned out to be great for the hotel. There were four seats in the middle of the boat, the bow rider would hold four people and there was a bench seat across the aft end. It was powered with a 450 horsepower in board Mercury engine. There was even a stereo system and a ship to shore radio. A customer mechanic replaced the ignition wires and spark plugs and charged the battery. It was like a new boat. Two German tourists at the hotel asked me where they could rent a boat for water skiing and I said to come with me. There was a beautiful owner's suite at the back of the property with a dock and my boat. I took them waterskiing a few times during their vacation. Gave them a water tour of Fort Lauderdale and a water taxi ride to an intercoastal restaurant. They told me that it was the best vacation they've ever had and wanted to know what they could bring for me next year. I ask for a bottle of German Rhine wine. They returned the following year with a case of wine. You might have guessed that they were both good-looking guys that wore spandex bathing suits. I am sure that I enjoyed them as much as they enjoyed the boat and the wine wasn't necessary. Logic dictates that good-looking guests are an asset to a gay resort, so I maintained the good business practice of entertaining good looking guests with the boat.

There was a knock on my door one afternoon and when I opened it, my first thought was there is a God. The guy standing in the doorway should have been a model or a movie actor. This tall, broad shouldered, blond in tight shorts wanted to talk to me. I wanted to say that I do my best listening in bed, but I exercised self restraint and simply invited him inside. His name was Jim S. and he had a gay baseball team. They wanted a sponsor. We already had a bowling team, a pool team, of volleyball team and a darts team that all produced increased revenues. We did sponsor the gay baseball team that quickly resulted in a Fort Lauderdale gay League involving six other bars.

I was sitting at the bar one afternoon and was quite sure that I knew the person sitting directly across from me, but I could not remember from where. It wasn't like me to approach somebody under these circumstances, but it bothered me to recognize this person and not know from where. So, I went over to him and said that I knew him from somewhere. I am the one who has always been careful because I feared rejection and this lack of judgment put me right where I did not want to be. He seemed very annoyed and acted as though I was making a pass at him. I returned to my seat and in a short time I heard him say the word Casa Lido to his friend. It immediately struck me that this was my old friend Ed, the bartender from the Casa Lido bar in Trenton. I was so glad to discover who it was because I could now go back and prove that I wasn't just making a pass at him. This time, he recognized me and his reaction was entirely different. It was easy for me to understand his defensive attitude because everyone hit on me as a bar owner. Some people would be friendly for a few minutes and then ask, "what is the chance of me getting a free drink". My stock answer was, "you have a better chance than I do because I paid for it when it came off the truck". Hustler boys would frequently be a problem because they were constantly bothering the customers for a drink, cigarette, or money. One of them sat next to me one night and he didn't realize who I was. He started with, "can I ask you a question". I said, "if you ask for a cigarette or a free drink, you will be thrown right out of here because we do not allow panhandling". His next question was, "can you tell me what time it is". We did allow some hustlers in the bar that were carefully screened because many of our guests were looking for that and we didn't want them going to some sleazy part of town and returning with somebody that would rob them. It was difficult to request police assistance because a hired prostitute stole his John's car, wallet and video camera.

There were two regular customers that were very annoying and I would escape through side doors to avoid them. They caught me at the bar one afternoon and asked if I was in a bad mood again. That was exactly the type of remark them made me avoid them. I told them that I did not have moods, but only reactions to whatever happens. If the lottery commission calls to tell me that I won, I would smile and be happy. If the dentist tells me that I need a root canal, I would not be very happy. If I am not happy when you are around, it is because you have the effect of a root canal on me.

Drugs, especially crack cocaine, were and continue to be a major problem in Fort Lauderdale. It seems like people can smoke crack cocaine one time and be destroy for life. There have been hundreds of nice looking, young straight guys that came to Fort Lauderdale and had to sell their bodies after becoming addicted to crack cocaine. I am sure that some of the old trolls have appreciated the fact that crack cocaine gives them a population of the young guys who will do anything for 20 bucks. Sexual desires make the old trolls overlook the fact that willingness to do anything for money is a very dangerous predicament for a business arrangement.

It is hard to know whether you should feel sorry for these kids or hate them. It is impossible to talk to them because they already know that they are destroyed by their addiction and cannot do anything about it. I hired a young guy to do maintenance work at the resort. His father was a carpenter and he was extremely talented in that field. He was also a really nice kid that you could enjoy as a good friend. Unfortunately, he was a really nice looking straight boy that you could use for any kind of perverted sex you might want because he was a crack addict. He had a great deal of respect for me in addition to the fact that I was physically capable of bouncing him around a room and I was determined to help him out of his addiction. My first Michael was an alcoholic and this Michael was a drug addict. I'm afraid to meet another Michael because I can't imagine the next step after drugs. He was in his late 20s and every dime that ever touched his hands had gone into drugs. When he admired a nice looking girl, I took advantage of the situation. I would tell him that most guys 10 years younger than him could take that girl out to dinner in their own car and maybe even wind up in their own apartment. Drugs have made it so that you could not even give her a cigarette if you walked to a coffee shop and she bought her own coffee. He knew that it was true and I could see that he did not want it to be true. I kept the pressure on him and he remained off the drugs for several weeks. One of our afternoon projects had us working in the hot sun for several hours. We went into the bar for a couple of cold beers and he wanted to follow up with a joint. He went outside and found one of his old friends that usually had a joint. I didn't stop him because I had been keeping him very restricted and felt that marijuana wasn't really that serious. What I didn't realize was that the beer was a bad decision in the first place and each buz was making him desire the next stronger drug. The D.J. booth was broken into and sound equipment was missing along with Michael. He returned after three days and slept for 24 hours. It was partly my fault because I started with the beer and I decided to try again. A few more weeks went by and everything was fine. I happen to stop in a pawnshop a few blocks from the resort and saw my DJ equipment. I couldn't prove anything because I didn't have the serial numbers, but it was unusual commercial grade equipment that had to be mine. I went back to the resort and made the managers write down the serial numbers of every piece of equipment that we owned. A short-time later, Michael asked me to buy an expensive saw for him to use in his carpentry work. The saw and Michael disappeared that night. He showed up a few days later and I told him that he wasn't welcome here anymore. He asked me if he could call his mother and I asked him for the number. I turned on my speaker phone and dialed her number. He told her that

143

he didn't have any place to stay and wanted to know if he could come home for a few nights until he found a place. She said "Michael, you were supposed to be helping me with the rent and every time you got a paycheck you would spend the next three days doing drugs and then come home broke. I could deal with that, but when you stole my wedding ring, that was the end. Then Michael reduced his request to one night. She said, "no fucking way ". If that was a mother's answer to her son, I was beyond my limitations in trying to help Michael. My father once said that the best thing to do with drug addicts, is put them on an island and give them as many drugs as they want. Michael was verifying the logic of dad's idea.

I went back to the pawn shop and found my saw. This time, I still had the purchase order with the serial numbers and told the owner that it was my stolen saw. He told me that he was tired of people trying to pull that kind of shit on him and I should get the hell out of the store. I told him that I wasn't pulling any shit and would gladly show him the purchase order with the serial numbers. He came out from behind the counter and pushed me out the door. I went home to pick up the purchase order on my way to get our local police officer. The officer and I returned to the pawn shop. The owner saw us coming across the parking lot and stopped us at the door. He pointed to me and told the policeman, "that son of a bitch already tried to rip me off and I will not let him in the store". Now he had made the cop mad. The officer said, "This gentleman is not going to rip you off with a policeman standing at his side, either you let us in or we will call for a search warrant and then let ourselves in." We went inside and matched up the serial numbers. The owner said to let him take the fucking thing. The policeman said, "No, he can't take it now because it is evidence. Your selling stolen merchandise and you have a police officer to testify that you were informed that it was stolen merchandise." The owner started saying that he was only trying to raise a family and had two kids at home to support. The policeman said, "now you want to be Mr. Nice Guy, we are done with you and you can try being Mr. Nice Guy to Bubba in jail tonight, I am sure that he will let you be his nice guy".

John got into a fight with my business partner, James. There was no way that I could possibly mend their differences. It resulted in our hiring a former bar owner as our bar manager. The new manager, Gary, was good at public relations and heavily involved with all of the sports people. He lost his own bar because he was terrible at money management and profit-making. We constantly got into arguments because he hired his gay friends for contracted services even though it was obvious that they were charging us four times the market value of their service. He suggested that we remove a kitchen from one of our bars and use the space for a shower room. The kitchen was equipped with expensive flame broilers, convection ovens, deep fryers, commercial dishwasher, walk-in refrigerator and freezer and a stainless steel hood system. The sale of kitchen equipment was supposed to cover the cost of installing showers and lockers. All of the equipment went and I never saw $1 from the sale. His gay plumber charged $400 to install two shower heads on existing plumbing from the old kitchen. His gay Carpenter charge $2,000 to install 8 ft. of lockers. When he hired somebody that I excluded from working for us, he would pay them with cash from the register. Whenever I challenged something done by Gary, he would have a long telephone conversation with my partner James and cause us to fight. He finally got another job offer and left us. A former restaurant owner, Bill, had been hired by Gary as an assistant. Bill assumed most of the duties that were being handled by Gary. Many former employees told me that they had quit because of Gary and would return as customers now that he had left. His new bar folded after a couple of years.

Bill was a functioning alcoholic. He drank vodka all day, but managed to stay sober until his work was finished. He did not manage to stay sober until he drove home and he received citations for driving while intoxicated. His personality was excellent for the job and it was fun to work with him. He was great with inspectors because his easy manor made inspectors overlook the minor violations that could have been reported. One night, he tried to go home and mistakenly drove up a service alley behind the motel. There was no exit and he tried to back out of the alley. His car slid down the back of the building and broke every water line going into the rooms. Our plumber worked all night making repairs. Bill did not report to work on the following day and one of the guests told me that the car which hit the building looked like Bill's. Sure enough, Bill finally showed up in his damaged car and admitted to hitting the building. He went to the veteran's hospital for assistance with his drinking problem and they put him on anabuse. The anabuse worked so well that he got sick if he put vinegar and oil on a salad. The fact that he couldn't drink caused him to use cocaine as a substitute. This was even worse because he wasn't functioning at all. Howard, the desk clerk, was doing the liquor purchases by taking the inventory sheets to Bill and returning an order to the vendors. Bill absolutely refused to come out of a motel room for days at a time.

Howard called me at home and said that a guest wanted to see the manager because a naked old man was standing outside on a balcony. I told him to call the manager, which was Bill. Howard said that he couldn't because it was the manager that was out on the balcony naked.

In recent years, Gary found someone to invest in another bar for him and it was successful because there was no competition left in Fort Lauderdale and the investor was controlling the money. During and immediately following the spring break era, everyone wanted to get into the gay bar business and it expanded to 54 bars advertising in the gay magazine. I was in the

Hideaway Gay bar one afternoon, talking to the owner. There were three other customers in this one time very popular bar. Jay, the owner, was reading the gay magazine and asked me if I realized that there were 54 gay bars. With his normal, dry sense of humor, he said that if we could get a few more gay bars he could thin this crowd down a little. One of the three customers left the room and I said that they must have opened another bar. The Bus Stop, Stanley's, Lefty's, the 825, I-beam, Boots, Buddy's, The Eagle, Sidestreet, Hideaway, Club Caribbean, BackStreets, Everglades, Whale and Porpoise, Gold Coast, The Saint, Lords, Rustler, Charms, The Curve, Tunnel Bar, Marlin Beach, Ends Up, January's, Sea Monster and more names than I can remember were all popular bars that closed before Gary's last bar opened. It didn't much matter what he did because it was one of the last watering holes in town except for 2 hustler bars, 2 leather bars, a few old queen's restaurants and some little neighborhood bars.

After Gary left, the disagreement between James and John had cooled down. John returned, but Gary had convinced James that we were stealing from the business and drunk all day. James started making regular trips to the bar and he did not know how to run a gay bar. He wanted the bartenders to wear white shirts and a black tie while a string quartet provided the entertainment. Our customers came to see Speedos and tank tops with disco music playing. James insisted that we close the famous "love Alley", a dark walkway between the back of the

148

motel and a concrete wall on the edge of the property. Love alley had a boardwalk, flower gardens and benches, but it was who went there and not what was there that made it popular. James had a girl that he was seeing in Florida. He would visit her every time he came to the club. James's wife, called the hotel to talk to James and the desk clerk thought it was the girlfriend. He said, "He isn't here, but I think he is on his way to your house", and he used the girlfriends name.

It eventually resulted in a divorce and James was in a bad situation because of his girlfriend. The club was put on the market for sale and we closed the business when an offer was made by a guy named Paton. Paton's deal fell apart and the closed club sat idle for a year. I had no idea what was happening until I was told that the bank foreclosed on the mortgage.

I continued to see John and he became mysteriously ill. Nobody was ever told what was affecting John, but he lost partial use of his arms and legs. He tried to write a name on a card for me and it looked like a 5 year old's handwriting. There were times when he would fall down and not be able to get back up. He told me that the hospital was checking for possible connections to his handling agent orange in the military, but they ruled that out. It became increasingly worse for about three months and he died.

Bill also had a sudden death, but it is known that he had a heart attack.

Chapter 20 - Looking Back

If there is life after death, all of my old friends are together and I am here almost alone. Thinking about that made me write down all of the names of people that I have lost.   The list was much longer than I would have realized and it made me feel like I was in the wrong place. Grandmom, mom, grandpop, Bud, and people that they never knew such as Philadelphia Frank, Scott the smiling bartender, my good friends John and Don and many, many more are all together, without me. Gay people need their gay friends because most of the world isn't home to gay people. Even though many have come out of the closet and fought for legal rights, society is still designed for heterosexual couples. I never really cared about the right to get married, in fact, I told some friends that I would just as soon have the right to shoot myself in the foot. The things that make a difference to me are not even noticed by most of our society, gay or straight. Movies have a happy ending when the leading man gets the good looking woman. A gay person doesn't see any value in getting a woman. Wasting a good looking man on a woman doesn't make a happy ending in the eyes of a gay person. Our happy ending would require ditching the bitch and making the switch. That would make us believe that the leading man won something worthwhile, but it isn't the way movies end. Not many straight people would enjoy movies that ended with the leading man matching up with another man.

Although working in a resort atmosphere made the work enjoyable, I am somewhat glad that it is gone. The business was successful enough to have made us wealthy if we had owned it in the 1960's, but everything was going to taxes and licensing fees in the late 1990's. I was working 14 hours a day to earn a quarter of a million dollars a year for the government. It is too bad that I couldn't apply the grandfather rule to taxes because the only tax that existed in 1943 was federal income tax and the quarter of a million was taxes in addition to income tax. The government claims that many of their taxes are charged to the tourists, but that is only true in theory. A tourist looks at the total amount they will be paying per night and couldn't care less how much of that goes to Florida Power and Light for electric, to the city for water, to the hotel staff for services or to the government for taxes. If the total amount is more than they would pay for a night in Cancun, they just go to Cancun. The resort was paying a 3% bed tax which would be used to build a stadium by the Everglades. We were in the business of selling entertainment and this 3% tourism tax meant that the government forced us to finance our competition. We were paying a liquor surtax that was instigated by mothers against drunk drivers and designed to keep drunks off of the highway. Our complex provided the only way for a group to have a drinking party together without driving because they could conclude their evenings by walking back to their motel rooms. A private house party would not be paying this surtax for their liquor even though every guest would need to drive home. I am happy that we were out of the business before the no-smoking laws came into existence because that would have been another unfair control. Nobody was forced to patronize the business and if someone didn't like smoking, they had the option of not entering our business place. We were the ones that had invested in the business and the only ones that could suffer a loss if it was managed poorly. It should have been our option to accommodate the clientele that we felt would be profitable, whether it be smokers or nonsmokers and if we made the wrong decision it would justifiably be our loss. Many businesses have either failed or suffered significant losses because of the non-smoking law and I can understand why. I once spent leisure hours walking through malls and would usually make some purchases. I seldom visit a mall anymore. Restaurant dining started with a glass of wine and a cigarette while waiting for the dinner entree. The new law makes me sit there uncomfortably wigging for a cigarette when I could be very comfortable at home. So, I stay home. We Americans tend to pat ourselves on the back and boast that we have freedom because we vote for our government. That is true in principle, but I would feel the reality of freedom if I could sit down in a restaurant, order a glass of white wine and light up a cigarette.

My generation saw the direct benefit of many freedoms which have been lost in an overcrowded world of laws and taxes. I truly

wonder if it would be worse to have a Queen
Elizabeth in the Whitehouse than to have lost all
of the freedoms that were once available in our
daily existence. I suppose it doesn't make much
difference because my retiring age has
eliminated the freedom of being able to start
over in a new place. I don't even feel very
welcome where I am because the world seems to
be a place for younger people. The beaches that
I enjoyed for so many years are far less
enjoyable without an athletic young body. Many
of the friends that shared my days of fun have
crossed over grandpops pedestrian bridge to the
cemetery. Not unlike the old burned church that
I was instrumental in replacing with a modern
and functional facility, the times, places, and
events that were my life are replaced by the
functioning world of the younger generation.

Most of my life is in the form of memories now,
so I spend my time writing them down for others
to know how it was for a different person in a
different time.

www.ingramcontent.com/pod-product-compliance
Lightning Source LLC
Chambersburg PA
CBHW020440290526
45785CB00002B/936